PRAISE FOR IN SEARCH OF A CO[illegible]

"Cladis has written an honest and [illegible] course after losing one's way. 'T[illegible] we must accept, even embrace,' h[illegible]nge is doing so in horrible weather. Throu[illegible]e, through divorce, through religious crisis, throug[illegible]essional and academic upheaval, through deep seated anxiety—Cladis charts his course so that we might weather life's seasons more gracefully."

—John Kaag, author of New York Times bestsellers, *American Philosophy: A Love Story*; *Hiking with Nietzsche: On Becoming Who You Are*; and *Sick Souls, Healthy Minds: How William James Can Save Your Life*

"What a rich feeling it is to fall under the spell of a truly compelling book. Mark S. Cladis layers introspective study with a thoughtful journey of personal loss and continuing discovery. His honesty and narrative grace combine with his gift for quoting from other writers to create a text of immense care and comfort. His long friendship with the poet/scholar Paul Kane shines as a bright thread tying the years together. A profound and meaningful book for students, teachers, people in transition, writers and friends—which is to say, everybody. I love it."

—Naomi Shihab Nye, Young People's Poet Laureate of the United States (Poetry Foundation)

"*In Search Of A Course* is a refreshingly ambitious and illuminating account of Cladis's impassioned confrontation with nothing less than the central questions of nature, religion, love, and education. This is a brave and important book."

—Ronald A. Sharp, acting president emeritus, Kenyon College; editor of *The Kenyon Review* emeritus; coeditor with Eudora Welty of *The Norton Book Of Friendship*

"Mark Cladis has written a heartfelt, affecting memoir of spiritual and intellectual discovery. Crushed by divorce and a midlife crisis, he sought a more authentic direction for both life and teaching during a long journey in the deserts of the Southwest under the guidance of poets, philosophers, Native American elders, and caring friends. He returned with new hope, new ideas, and a transformed vision of both life and work. This book will speak to anyone who cares about spirituality and education, especially those who have struggled to gracefully weave heart, mind, family, and home place together."

—John Tallmadge, author and essayist on nature and culture, past president of the Association for the Study of Literature and Environment and director of the Orion Society.

"In higher education, we sometimes talk about the liberal arts as learning to think while we feel and to feel while we think. Mark Cladis's *In Search of a Course* is a stunning example of what such integrative work actually looks and feels like—in all the vulnerability, pain, joy and collective self-discovery this searching entails."

—Samuel Speers, D. Min, Dean for Religious and Spiritual Life and Contemplative Practices, Vassar College

In Search of a Course

Lessons in Life, Learning, and the Environmental Imagination

Mark S. Cladis

Pact Press

Published by Pact Press
An imprint of
Regal House Publishing, LLC
Raleigh, NC 27612
All rights reserved

https://pactpress.com

Printed in the United States of America

ISBN -13 (paperback): 9781646030132
ISBN -13 (epub): 9781646030408
Library of Congress Control Number: 2020930421

Interior and cover design by Lafayette & Greene
lafayetteandgreene.com
Cover images © by Victoria Lipov/Shutterstock

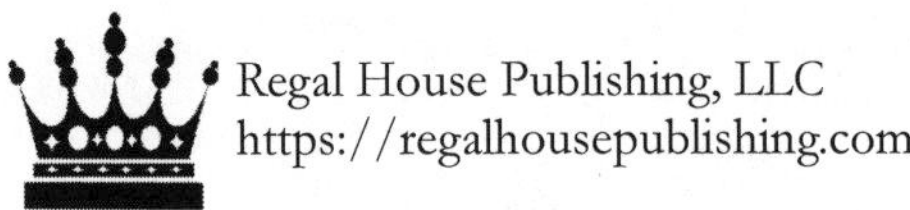

Regal House Publishing, LLC
https://regalhousepublishing.com

Printed in the United States of America

To Mina and Paul, bestowers of the strength of love

There is a comfort in the strength of love;
'Twill make a thing endurable, which else
Would overset the brain, or break the heart…

–William Wordsworth

Part I

In Search of a Course

Day One

Flight from New York to Albuquerque

"If you want, we can probably send your bags up by Yellow Taxi. They should get to Santa Fe by 7:00 this evening."

This is what the cheerful Delta Air agent said to Paul and me about our lost luggage the morning we arrived in Albuquerque. This is how we came to embark on our journey with only assorted toiletries and one change of clothes between us. It is how we began our search for a course.

Obstacles are often an ingredient in rites of passage, and ours was to be no different. Paul and I, a poet and a philosopher, had traveled to the Southwest to gather material for a course we planned to teach the following semester at Vassar College, where we worked as professors. The course, *It's Only Natural: Contemplation in the American Landscape*, would explore various philosophical, religious, and historical approaches to the natural world in American traditions, and especially in Native American cultures. Paul and I had come two thousand miles to learn from two people we believed could be of help: Lorain Fox Davis, a Cree and Blackfeet healer who lives in southern Colorado, and Benjamin Barney, a Navajo (Diné) educator who lives in Arizona. That morning in the airport, we did not know yet how many more teachers we would recruit along the way.

But I had my own reasons for being in Albuquerque that day: namely, to flee the crisis that had beset me back home. My life as I knew it—replete with the love of spouse, vocation, and Spirit—had crumbled. Yes, I was a professor of religious studies, teaching courses on spirituality, religious culture, and the natural world. I had received a doctorate and a Master of

Divinity, published several books, numerable essays and reviews, and had taught at elite colleges around the country. I was, one might say, a "seasoned" scholar who claimed to teach on the art of living. But when my own spiritual foundation gave way, I was wholly unprepared to rebuild it. Self-confidence, love of self, trust in life, belief in what and how I taught—these supports had deserted me. I needed guidance and not the academic or intellectual sort. I needed open air, a change of scene, a friendship, and an education.

Professionally, what was I searching for? My search on behalf of the college and my students was for answers to such questions as: What are meaningful philosophical, religious, and aesthetic approaches to the land? What is the relation between inner and outer landscapes? How does the land nourish the environmental imagination, and how does the environmental imagination nourish a sense of the land? Ultimately, the professional search led to such implausibly large questions as: What is home, beauty, and love, and how do these connect to the land?

These questions, in turn, prompted basic institutional questions: Is it appropriate to approach such expansive questions in the contemporary research university or liberal arts college? Is there a place in the university or college for such practical inquiries as "How shall we live?" or for such Socratic quests as "Know thyself"? What is education, anyway? There was a time in my life when these questions wouldn't have occurred to me, but now they, too, had become part of the search for a course.

Personally, what was I searching for? Answers to some of life's more haunting perplexities, especially those that pertain to Location and Direction: Where was I? How did I get here? Where was I headed? Was I to accept my location—dispossessed of a loving marriage and of self-confidence in my vocation? Was I to protest it? Fight to restore everything as it once had been? In order to move on, I needed to understand the relationship between acceptance and protestation in the process of change so I could move from dense darkness to a more promising land, from the painful loss of love to its redemptive presence.

So I traveled to the Southwest in search of a course—one for my college, which included my colleague, Paul, and one for myself, on my own, as I sought to rebuild my life.

The search began in the airport. The lost baggage may have been inconvenient, yet it was distinctly fitting for us and our journey. Picking up some things can require letting go of others. On some journeys, we need to embark unencumbered, or at least begin the process of letting go. Indeed, sometimes learning to let go *is* the journey.

Paul and I spent that afternoon in William Clift's photography studio in Santa Fe. Bill is an American photographer, celebrated especially for his black-and-white images of landscapes in New Mexico. Bill and Paul had been collaborating on a book that sought to bring together verse and photography. Bill's gelatin silver prints have brought him many awards and fellowships, and his work is featured and included in the collections of such places as the J. Paul Getty Museum in Los Angeles, the Metropolitan Museum of Art in New York, and the Saint Louis Art Museum. Once you meet him, however, you quickly realize that he is entirely uninterested in the standard measures of professional success. Above all, he is committed to honest *work*: to a patient way of looking at the world, capturing (an aspect of) that world, and then asking, "So, what do *you* see?"

Since we were in the area, it seemed natural that Paul and I pay him a visit. We drove up, parked in the short driveway of the famous landscape photographer's modest home, and knocked on the front door. I was still thinking about my lost baggage (How would I brush my teeth? What if I needed a sweater?) when a pair of eyes appeared, so piercing and perceptive as to silence these thoughts of lost things. I realize it's predictable to comment on the eyes of a world-class photographer, but I can hardly pretend that Bill's eyes were not remarkable—wide and searching like the lens of the Brownie camera he used as a ten-year-old on Beacon Hill in Boston. I have only vague memories of his chiseled, Rockwellesque face; those eyes of his have erased most other recollections of his appearance. But I know this: I could recognize him forty years from now by only his eyes.

Instead of welcoming us into his home, Bill led us behind it and through a small, tidy backyard to what looked like a windowed shed, which was his studio. Thus far, everything about Bill's home seemed quite ordinary: a smallish house, yard, and outbuilding. I have no complaint against the commonplace. That's where I live. But I expect different surroundings from famous prodigies, of people like Bill—who, at the age of fifteen, took his first photography workshop with one of America's foremost landscape photographers, Paul Caponigro, and whose prints are now recognized as among the most masterful in the world.

As we entered Bill's studio, however, the ordinary quickly gave way to the astonishing. Imagine entering a shack and discovering an artist's laboratory, a lifetime's accumulation of tools and aesthetic predilections, a space where everything is perfectly placed, designed, crafted. The lighting was bright but not glaring. The wood floors were clean but not glossy. The room was a workshop built with precision and meticulousness, yet it was neither cold nor sterile. It was a Shaker Society built for one. I would not have been surprised to hear, upon entering the threshold of that sturdy, handsome room, the voice of Ann Lee: *Do your work as though you had a thousand years to live and as if you were to die tomorrow.* Patience and urgency both resounded within those walls. It brought a new perspective to my own struggles, for I was beginning to understand that my path, too, would require patience and urgency in equal measure.

Let me tell you a story about a man who discovers entirely by accident that his life has led him into a storm that he may not survive. He now realizes that there had been warning signs of the impending disaster, and he experiences the bitter self-reproach of retrospective knowledge. But none of this changes the fact that on this day he is blindsided by the realization of tragedy. Until now, he had nurtured the illusion that his was one of the happier marriages, that his wife's frequent crying episodes—especially those after meetings with her therapist—were the sobs of past pain, grief, and disappointment, not tears of confusion, misery, and despair over her current life and marriage.

These are some of the details that friends have said I absolutely must supply. *How can you write about your trip to the Southwest and not mention the calamity that precipitated it?* In *My Past and Thoughts* Herzen writes, "Man likes to enter into another existence, he likes to touch the subtlest fibers of another's heart, and to listen to its beating…."[1] The details of my past existence, however, seem strangely unimportant to me. The gale arrived and I capsized. This has happened to most of us at least once in our lives. We know this experience intimately without my offering any "subtle fibers" of my own. And yet there rings my friends' rejoinders: "But each person's story is particular and its power and hope is in the telling. Tell us what happened. Tell the story."

Are the details too trivial and unimportant or too painful and personal? It is convenient to write abstractly about past pain: it fosters the illusion that future pain might be felt theoretically, not acutely. I will tell the story. If I am to write this book, I must. And when I reveal intimate things, I will cling to the belief that "there are things so deeply personal that they can be revealed only to strangers."[2]

While my wife, Deirdre, was in Minneapolis visiting a friend, I went to a movie with the mathematician John McCleary, a Vassar colleague and friend. Deirdre and I had been married now for about twelve years. Although we usually traveled to places together, occasionally one of us would make a trip on our own. That's what happened this time. Deirdre went to Minneapolis, and I went to the movie.

The film was *The Perfect Storm,* and, as fate would have it, it would be the state of my life over the next twelve months. As I sat watching George Clooney play the captain of a fishing boat who unwittingly leads his shipmates into a catastrophic storm, I realized that I, too, was about to encounter life-threatening waves. Looking back, it was all rather remarkable. There I was, in the middle of this action movie when, out of the blue, certain details of my life and marriage began to surface and churn in my mind, synthesizing spontaneously into a vision of truth as lucid and clear as it was heartbreaking and ruinous. The mysterious canceled train tickets, the nebulous late-night support group in distant White Plains, the hushed phone calls, the secret internet chat rooms, the private room that all but explicitly decreed, DO NOT ENTER, and her tearful and taciturn presence—all these pieces of Deirdre's life suddenly came together in the darkness of the movie theater and fashioned in my heart the message, *Your life is in danger.*

There are storms in our lives that we can name and track. We watch them slowly emerge and take shape. We may not be certain of their exact trajectory or potential force, but we nonetheless have some warning of the danger ahead. Sometimes we are proactive and take wise measures to minimize the damage. Other times we are complacent and attempt to ride it out. And then there are the storms that come with no warning, whose signs perhaps are veiled or unavailable. In these cases, we fancifully wish we had an early-warning system to alert us of those imminent winds approaching to topple our lives. We desire a crystal ball. An itinerary. But how much warning would we need? How much time? Twenty-four to forty-eight hours are usually sufficient for people to prepare or to evacuate their homes before an approaching storm. Yet how many hours do you need to prepare for the news that your spouse has made arrangements to leave you?

When the film was over John asked if I wanted to go out for a beer. He couldn't have known of my quiet internal drowning beside him or of my desperation to get home. The credits were still rolling as I raced homeward, hoping that if I could discern the direction and force of the approaching winds—if I could understand more fully the forecast—I might track this storm. I might name it. I might deter it.

Bill Clift's prints, which had taken twenty-five years of photographic study and which we spent the next three hours examining, were magnificent. Their subject was Shiprock, a massive geological formation known as a volcanic neck or plug—the remains of a solidified lava core of a dormant volcanic pinnacle. Shiprock rises out of the Colorado Plateau—"the Land of Room Enough and Time"—its shape and majesty akin to the cathedral at Chartres. Located in the Navajo Nation in the northwest corner of New Mexico, it is a sacred site to the Navajo—and to others as well. The French social theorist Emile Durkheim deemed that anything could be held deeply sacred by a people—a worm or weed, a stump of a tree or stone underfoot. The sacredness of an object, according to Durkheim, has nothing to do with inherent worth or value. Rather, it all depends on what a group happens to value. The sacred worm of the Worm People, then, isn't intrinsically sacred; it is made sacred by the collective, reflective representations of the people. Yet Shiprock reminds us of what we intuitively know and what Durkheim neglected: some things and places are *intrinsically* remarkable and, like gravity, attract us and hold us in place. See Shiprock and be struck with wonder—whoever you are, wherever you are. It's really that simple.

This is not to say that Shiprock is not also an idea, a storied landscape, what some would call a social construction. It has emerged as much from the material of culturally specific beliefs and sensibilities as from the deep volcanic matter under the desert. The *Navajo* Shiprock, then, is higher and deeper and more substantial than my own. For the Navajo, it is both an intimate and a fearsome place, steeped in layers of historical, traditional, and mythological meaning.

In part, I came to the desert to learn from Shiprock how to be quiet, resolved, and at peace. In the midst of crisis, I sought the strength and majesty the mountain seemed to offer. Its slopes had withstood eons of natural and cultural change, had acquired and lost many narratives, had seen its pilgrims arrive at and depart this earth. Yet from the mountain I received little in the way of answers or insights. The rock stayed mostly silent, and I understood that I was not entirely welcome. It was not my place. At best, I was a visitor with a short-term, limited visa.

Still, my relation to Shiprock has not been static. In time it has changed and deepened. To this day, each morning when I face west, I conjure Shiprock. My initiation began not at Shiprock itself nor with the Navajos, but in Bill's studio. Studying his photographs, I began to acquire some insight—or at least a glimpse of Bill's sight. Each print contained some perceptive account of Shiprock, some rendering, some unselfish response.

What did I see? How did my initiation begin? As Bill patiently presented print after print, his work encouraged nascent questions, indistinct wonderings, remote echoes, faint dawns over new landscapes. Wittgenstein once remarked that where a trained eye will see something clearly, "a weak eye will see a blurred patch of color."[3] In those black-and-white photographs, I saw blurred patches. My eyes were weak but I knew enough not to try too hard to see clearly, lest I lose my ability to see at all. The photos required that I yield to them, that I accept what I *could* see. Eventually, images, patterns, emotions, ideas, and judgments did begin to emerge, if dimly. The massive rock that had at first appeared as an implacable monolith began to shift shapes: gentle and quiet in one moment, fierce and threatening in another; playful and youthful here, wise and aged there. As we studied more prints, in different seasons, lightings, and angles, Shiprock the monolith gave way to Shiprock the matrix, the mother cradling countless distinct progeny of stone, one face within another, each hewn from the same ancient rock. As if opening an intricate, ecclesial nesting doll, Bill had exposed the graceful chapels housed within this stone cathedral.

Did Bill's photographs discover, or did they produce that stony world I looked upon? Did they reveal or create? This polarizing academic question seemed inappropriate then and even more so now. Ansel Adams said correctly, "You don't take a photograph, you make it." But I'm sure he also meant to say, "You don't take the land, it makes you."

To view the work of one who has spent over twenty-five years photographing the same site was to begin to understand how a skillful artist both listens and speaks to a place. Love and respect require the same—and these, too, I saw in Bill's work. There was also a trace of the suffering that must accompany honest, patient work. Mostly, though, I saw in those prints a lifelong conversation between man and stone. Bill had done most of the listening. After all, he had spoken with a mountain.

The house was dark when I returned from the movie. The garage door opener didn't work, and I remember my hands trembling as I struggled to unlock the front door. Once inside the house, I headed straight for my wife's special space—that secretive room at the back of the house in which she spent most of her time. At the threshold of the room, I recollected a conversation we'd had months earlier about rearranging the house for the potential arrival of a baby. She made it clear that "her room" was not to be touched or altered. It occurred to me as I stood in front of her room that she had seemed excessively protective, territorial even, of her private sanctuary. At the time it sounded entirely reasonable, but now it became another piece of ominous evidence—what was she hiding in there?

It took me about two minutes to discover what would upend my world. Slips of paper, more canceled train tickets, her diary, candles, tarot cards, and the hidden books: evidence of extramarital affairs—past, present, and future—and of occult practices intended to produce romantic love outside our marriage. It was becoming clear why this room was shrouded in secrecy. Was I a fool for not entering earlier? Should I have grasped the strangeness of my exclusion from this room in our home? Regardless, it was clear now. I had made a terrible discovery, but in so doing I had become a prowler, a trespasser of private space. That deed would become an indigestible stone in my stomach that I would forever carry with me.

All night long, I was gripped by panic. My wife was not who I thought she was, which meant my life was not what I thought it was. Everything around me—that auburn shirt she had worn the morning I took her to the airport, her tourmaline hairbrush in the bathroom, the mango yogurt in the refrigerator, the green flip flops in the entryway—every corner, shelf, room, and hallway, which had moments earlier held the stuff of the ordinary and the comfortable, suddenly bore artifacts of the incongruous and the terrifying. It all brought a piercing stab to my heart, for everything in the home was intimately connected to her, and she had suddenly become a stranger to me. Nothing, I knew, would ever be the same.

At four in the morning I made the phone call to Minneapolis. The apartment mate of Deirdre's friend answered the call:

"Yes, I know it is late. I'm terribly sorry. But may I speak to my wife? It's rather urgent," I said.

"She hasn't returned this evening. She's still out with friends," was her reply.

"Please, please leave her a note and ask her to call me when she returns."

By the time my pathetic call was returned two hours later, I was sobbing. I told her that I thought we were going to grow old together. I told her that I thought that she was my life partner, that we were two peas in a pod. With much vulnerability and tenderness, I expressed to Deirdre my terror that she no longer loved me, that she loved others, and that she sought to leave me. My words were as surreal as they were distressing. Was I actually speaking them? Hours earlier, I would not have believed that I would ever in my life make utterances of such disbelief and sadness.

I was desperate for some simple words of comfort from my wife, some indication that my fears were unfounded, some lucid explanation. *Mark, why are you so upset? What has happened? Calm down—everything's okay, of course it is.* Instead, I received silence and then vagueness. "Let's talk when I get home. I'm tired now. It's hard for me to think straight." I should have understood then the situation was hopeless, but hope—if hope it was—can be the hardest thing to let go.

Over the next couple of months I would sometimes watch myself cry in the mirror. It was more an act of curiosity and confirmation than of self-pity. *Whose face is this? So swollen, moist, and dark. This is the face of sadness. This is your face.* Occasionally, I would hide in the car in the darkness of the garage and weep.

In those moments, I was constructing for myself a hideout from a world that had inflicted such pain on me—a world of attachment, failed love, and stark and sudden disillusionment. I was seeking a sanctum where I could hide and heal in solitude. But there was no sanctuary from inner pain in the locked car, the dark closet, or the empty office. Real sanctuary, I would learn, is a place populated by other people—family members, teachers, students, friends.

❧

I met Paul Kane almost exactly ten years before my marriage began to fall apart. We had both arrived at Vassar College that year; he was forty years old, and I was thirty-two. We both served on the Student Fellowship Committee, a group of faculty that gives various awards to deserving students. At the committee's large conference table, Kane was always impeccably poised—neither slouched nor forced, always upright and relaxed. In those days, he was fair-complexioned, clean-shaven, and nearly six feet tall, with dark brown hair worn short. (Today his hair is silvery gray, and—don't ask me how—he is at least an inch taller.) If ever someone looked like a New England Yankee, it was Paul Kane—though he was born and raised in Schoharie County, upstate New York. Urbane, cultured, and mild-mannered, Kane was at home in the high arts and literary culture of Manhattan, at openings for invited guests at the Met and readings at the New York Society Library. Raised in the less tailored world of Northern California, I took note of Paul's genteel profile above his white starched shirt and fine Merino sweater—on a warm day, no less.

I couldn't have known, then, with my West Coast conception of New England and its culture of refinement, that Paul Kane was no poster child of urbanity. Paul is as comfortable with manual labor as he is with Harold Bloom and Joseph Brodsky—in fact, he worked as a carpenter for many years before I met him. He is as likely to be seen building a barn as writing a poem. I don't mean to suggest merely that he is multitalented or, worse, "multifaceted" in the way of interests. I wish to identify an inner complexity—a complexity that no doubt derives from and relates to that *something* in Paul that has ineffably attracted, but unfailingly escaped, me. If my California skepticism had pegged Paul as staid, decorous, and proper, the surprise over the years has been to learn the depths of his whimsical, mischievous, and even illicit nature.

Around that large conference table, among mostly fidgety faculty members, Paul sat relaxed and practically motionless—except for his lively eyes. His hazel eyes, like Emerson's "transparent eyeball," seemed both to behold and to reveal. Paul watched with an attentiveness that disclosed a vibrant alertness, and his speech, when he spoke, was equally intense and sensitive. He posed something of a mystery to me.

We served on the Fellowship Committee together for our first two years at Vassar and both took yearlong sabbaticals in our third year. I didn't give Kane a thought while on sabbatical and had all but forgotten his enigmatic character by the time I returned to the college the next fall. Shortly after my return, however, I was perusing the campus directory for a colleague to take to lunch, saw Kane's name, and considered calling his office.

Think of those pivotal moments of chance or grace that helped you on your way: when that patient teacher offered exactly the guidance you needed; when the doctor ordered the life-saving laboratory test; when you turned down a ride home in that car that would careen fatally off the highway; when you walked to your office at that particular hour of the day, on that particular route, and you first met the one who would become your life partner—the one with whom you would have children and grow old. How many moments of grace have we received, and how many have we declined? I can't help but wonder now how close I came that day to moving on, to bypassing Kane's name and missing an event that would forever change my life.

I called Paul Kane.

We met at the Dutch Cabin and ordered Mexican. After a meal of fajitas and friendly conversation, Paul asked, "Where should we eat next week?" *Next week?* What a remarkable question! What a great presumption! But in asking, Paul had made a statement, a deliberate choice to see past our frenzied schedules and commit to something simple and social, and he was challenging me to do the same. I sometimes think Paul knew that if we met the next week, we would continue to meet every week for a decade—and we did. People's lives are transformed by near-death experiences, the arrival of children, the departure of loved ones. Mine was unmistakably and irreversibly altered by a lunch invitation.

After sampling the menu and atmosphere of a few restaurants within walking distance of Vassar, Paul and I became regulars at Stacey's coffee shop, Cobbablu. Eventually we paid our "dues" to Stacey a year in advance, so there was no reaching for the wallet after the meal. At some point we stopped ordering—Stacey just brought us food and gratefully we ate. Some habits and rituals lull us into thoughtlessness, cause us to become forgetful of why we do what we do. Others, however, can make us more fully awake. They can provide a routine and opportunity for the practice of reflection and consideration—a ritual, in this case, that offered not heavenly salvation but a measure of earthly equanimity. It also offered a friendship that would eventually save my life. Perhaps, then, something of the divine was offered.

Deirdre and I continued to live together in the house. I suppose we still loved each other, even though the marriage was gradually expiring in every way except legally. When she returned from Minneapolis, the day after my phone call, I continued for a few days to seek words of comfort and a clear assertion that my fears were groundless. As before, I mainly received silence and ambiguous assurances. I was asking the impossible from her, a fact I must have known then but denied to both of us.

Less than a week after her Minneapolis trip, I was outside gathering eggs from the hens and preparing to tend to the bees. She met me at the bee yard, poised to help. I turned to her, both of us beneath the white hoods of our strange beekeeping suits, and said, "These bees, those chickens, the wood lot, the raspberry patch, our home, our life—it's all changed. *Everything* is different now. *Nothing* is the same."

For months to come I would cycle through the Kübler-Ross stages of grief, sometimes experiencing all of them within a single day—denial, anger, bargaining, and depression—every stage except the last one, acceptance.

❧

Emerson wrote, "A nobler want of man is served by nature, namely, the love of Beauty."[4] Many of us believe this. I know I do. Humans have a need, a longing, for beauty. The marvels of the natural world—seen nakedly or through, say, a microscope—can nurture and address this desire for beauty. This seems clear enough. But Emerson went on to write, "Beauty in nature is not ultimate. It is the herald of inward and eternal beauty."

For Emerson, the beauty of the natural world—whether of a particular tract of land or of the entire physical universe—never stands alone. It is always connected to something larger. But what could possibly be larger than the physical universe? Emerson answers: Spirit. Spirit infuses and sustains all things, all relations, all processes in time and space. Spirit is immanent and thus is called inward. Yet it is also transcendent and thus is called eternal. And one of the chief messengers of inward, eternal Spirit is the beauty of the natural world. An expanse of land, then, can be a herald angel announcing over and over, in different ways to different people, the presence of Spirit. Did Shiprock announce to Bill Clift this Presence? Was Bill listening for something beyond Shiprock?

The land possesses its own beauty, no doubt, but its particular beauty points beyond itself—even as it participates in that to which it points. This gesturing beyond must be Emerson's reason—his only excuse—for qualifying or relativizing the beauty of the natural world. And Emerson was surely right to add the qualifier. One can reject his notion of Spirit and still acknowledge that the land is one among many concentric circles of things and of life, overlapping and crisscrossing here and there, but ultimately and always interrelated. Beauty—whether of the land, of an institution, or of an action—is never in isolation. It has its own integrity, but it also reflects and draws on a larger Whole.

But I must wonder, did Emerson move too quickly from a singular instance of beauty to eternal beauty? Don't we need to linger with our particular messengers of beauty before leaving them behind for something larger? The beauty that captures our attention—this rose or that desert mountain—calls on us to move both toward and beyond it. But perhaps moving in the direction of the Whole does not always require that we leave particular beauty behind.

My sense was that Bill Clift was willing to linger in the beauty. For the time being, he was satisfied to sit with Shiprock. I can't say whether his mountain—surely a universe unto itself—was also leading him to a still larger mountain, an encompassing matrix. I simply didn't know enough to wonder, "And beyond Shiprock?" But I knew this: Bill's messenger was as legion as its messages. It is a mistake to think beauty is singular or necessarily pretty or soothing. Beauty can terrify and unsettle. It can wake us up and thrust us into newness and fear. It is as likely to injure as it is to heal.

This is how Shiprock came to work on me. In Bill's studio, with my hands full of his prints, it was as if I'd been wounded, pierced corporally by an aching question the images woke in me. Shiprock inspired broad notions: the way it imposes its own vast geological time zone which shrinks the self and places it in an ocean of time that leads back to creation. Shiprock's impassive presence holds infinite shapes and embraces constant change and drama. These themes are enough to feed on for a lifetime. Yet below or above them still whispered the call for a response, or so I thought.

When we first arrived in Albuquerque, its dry air and bright sun, its droughty trees and brushy plants stirred memories and intimations of a former home—Palo Alto, California. Palo Alto, of course, is no desert. But in July it shares more in common with the Southwest than with the place I called home at the time of my crisis: the green, dense, humid Hudson River Valley of New York. In my youth in California, I would hike among the shrub oaks and tall golden grasses, often with camera in hand, attempting to capture the beauty, longing, and disquiet the landscape stirred in me. In my makeshift darkroom in the downstairs bathroom, the images that emerged disappointed. Some were pretty, some interesting, yet none offered what I asked of it: to tame the wildness by catching it on film, to arrest and eternalize the beauty that so moved me.

One black-and-white photograph came close. It was framed by two dark, lichen-covered oak trees that inclined gently inward, as if to form a Gothic arch, while bands of bright light led the eye over the grassy foreground toward a winding path. The print was almost perfectly self-contained. Yet the path, like most paths, led away, out of sight, and this "disappearing line" rendered the photograph somehow boundless or incomplete. The photograph didn't offer closure or conclusion but presented a fundamental mystery, a question perhaps about my own incompleteness and future wanderings. I did not have the artistic assurance of Bill Clift or William Wordsworth, for whom the open path "was like a guide into eternity."[5]

What strikes me now is that even then I was haunted by an indefinable question—whose answer lay in the very journey of working out the question itself. And so, the old quest became part of the new.

Two weeks after I entered my wife's secret room, while Deirdre was away, I found myself holding my hunting rifle. I was on the phone with Paul's wife, Tina, and trying to explain how my spiritual foundation—those ideals, principles, and ethical practices to which I had devoted my personal and professional life—were not holding up in my time of need. I sobbed as I described to her the feel of the cold barrel of the hunting rifle against my head. I told her I only wanted to know what it was like, to feel it against me as my body seethed with the heft of lamentation. Tina kept me on the phone for the hour it took Paul to make the sixty-mile trip from his house to mine. Only after he pulled into my driveway and had taken away my guns did she hang up.

I used to own chickens. I would order hens but sometimes one or two turned out to be roosters and I'd need eventually to slaughter them. It would take me a couple of days to prepare emotionally for this necessary yet violent act—in this case, to play the part of the butcher, the hawk, or the fox. At one of our weekly lunch meetings years before, I asked Paul if he could slaughter a chicken or shoot a deer. Many environmentalists, after all, value direct participation with local, non-corporate, sustainable food. I remember well Paul's firm but nonjudgmental response. He laughed gently, shook his head, and said in a low voice, "No, absolutely not." Not surprisingly, Paul never owned a firearm.

Yet that night, he passed through the dark woods with my guns in his arms. Once at Vassar, he crossed the campus to his office and locked them inside.

Imagine—the gentle poet carrying a 12-gauge shotgun and a .30-06 rifle over the manicured grounds of Vassar College. It's another image of the paradox of Kane, so mild-mannered, so shamelessly bold. An image of care and friendship. Of moral dilemma. He would not put the guns in his car, nor would he store them in his home. But they must, unquestionably, be removed from my house. So off he went on foot from my home to Vassar College. The potential headlines must have run through Paul's mind: *Vassar Professor Stalks Campus Armed. Student Discovers Pacifist's Hidden Gun Stash During Office Hours. Poet Risks Career for Friend.*

Paul's responses to moral dilemmas have often surprised me. Once when his good friend, the dean of the faculty, asked Paul to meet with him, Paul worried that he would be asked to become Chair of the English department. Navigating the power and politics of that position was unthinkable for Paul, and yet saying no to a friend was equally unacceptable. So what did he do? He started looking for another teaching job outside Vassar. (Luckily for everyone, the dean had never intended to ask him to become Chair.)

Around 7:30 p.m. our luggage arrived by Yellow Taxi at Bill's studio. It had caught up with us, making its claim. The taxi driver hoisted Paul's bag out of the trunk and said, "Just one bag, right?" My heart sank. My bag was nowhere in sight. "No, two!" I exclaimed, and the driver laughed. "That gets them every time," he said, hauling my bag from the backseat.

Every time. I don't doubt it. The driver has had much experience with travelers and our attachments, with all those things we think we can't live without. Like crows, we "pick up everything that glitters, no matter how uncomfortable our nests get with all that metal in them."[6] If Bill's Shiprock granted me a moment of immense perspective that managed to lighten my load, the Yellow Taxi driver reminded me of my near compulsive need to encumber my life—to face the world with baggage in hand. How to let go? What to let go of? And, in the midst of all that disenthralling, what to keep? These questions, too, became part of the search.

It was a quiet evening as we left Bill's studio and drove north from Albuquerque to Crestone, Colorado, where we were to meet Lorain Fox Davis. The names of the towns on Highway 285 were as foreign to me as the flora in that arid landscape: Pojoaque, Velarde, Tres Piedras, Alamosa; scrawny junipers, desert shrubs, cactus, bunch grass. Towns and plants alike were at home in the struggle to survive in that parched land. By the time we skirted the eastern edge of the San Juan Mountains, the sky was dark, and silence filled our rental car. By now, Paul and I had been meeting for lunch once a week for many years. We'd learned how to accept quietness in each other's company.

We continued north on Highway 285 and stopped near Los Pinos to call Lorain Fox Davis and tell her we would arrive late, probably past midnight. When I told her about the lost baggage she laughed softly. Although I had yet to meet her, I imagined her smiling knowingly, as if to say, yes, this is often needful.

As we crossed the state line into southern Colorado and drove north of Alamosa, I suppose we both conjectured about Lorain—about who she was and what work she would do with us. It's something of an act of faith to spend three days with a stranger—sleeping and eating and learning together in an isolated house on a wide plateau. Mark Wallace, a friend and fellow philosopher of religion at Swarthmore College, first told us about Lorain. He had participated in one of her workshops on Native American traditions. The workshop was sponsored by Naropa, Boulder's alternative university dedicated to contemplative education. At Naropa, as in Crestone, East meets West—not the Yankee–Gaucho encounter, but more of an Ancient India–Classical Greece variety. "Lorain is terrific," Mark told me. "She knows and lives her Blackfeet and Cree traditions, and she is *generous*." His comments about Lorain were apt, and I suspect now that generosity characterizes all skillful educators.

By now we had been heading north from Santa Fe for about four hours. At Moffat, fifty miles north of Alamosa, we turned east. *East.* If my West Coast roots had made me regard the Northeast as the direction of cultural refinement and Yankee stereotypes, I saw East—the direction of dawn—as the path to hope, new beginnings, new challenges. So I believed, driving east through the dark of southern Colorado.

My perfect storm had hit in early August, about a year before our journey into the desert. Shortly after its impact, Paul said we needed to get me in shape for the semester that would begin within the month. I realize now that Paul's modes of rescue were unusual. A week after my crisis began, a rare F4 tornado cut a large swath through Poughkeepsie, and Paul volunteered us to clear the yard of an English professor who had been trapped in her house by fallen trees. With chainsaw in hand,

I cut feverishly through the wood, working simultaneously through my own pain and frustration.

About a week later, Paul showed up at my house in his blue Toyota mini-truck with an old mattress in the back. I looked at him dubiously and thought, What, *another* dumpster run? Reading my mind, he said simply, "That's right." There was some construction underway at the Vassar student housing complex. We drove to campus, unloaded the truck bed, and, in broad daylight, heaved the old mattress into an already overflowing dumpster. Before the mattress had even landed on the heaping trash pile, a construction worker began shouting and running toward us in protest. Like any sensible professors in the presence of students, we jumped in the mini-truck and screeched into the street. The man continued to chase us, shouting, before eventually losing ground. From beginning to end, the adventure brought us excitement, fear, and laughter. Within moments of escape, Paul and I looked at each other and bellowed in unison, "VERSE"—the word printed in bold all-caps on Paul's personalized New York license plate. Neither the students nor workers could possibly have missed it.

The mischievous poet was willing to turn us into criminals for the sake of my health and happiness. Paul cared for me, dedicated time to me, took risks for me. I had told Tina, his wife, that my spiritual foundation was crumbling when I needed it most. Paul shored up that foundation. He didn't substitute himself for it, offer himself up to save me from descent. Neither of us would have tolerated that. His gifts to me were more substantial, more selfless. He accompanied me through my most turbulent times, offering me a chance to rebuild.

When I think back on Paul's care during my calamity, all that beauty in motion, actions both playful and serious, there is one image of Paul that I insist on holding onto. In the January that followed my fateful August, with plenty of snow on the ground and a full, cold moon in the sky, Paul and I embarked on another illicit, life-affirming journey: climbing Mohonk Mountain on cross-country skis at midnight. When we had ascended halfway up the mountain, snow began to fall on us from the bright sky with its westerly moon. As I paused to watch the flakes dance in the cold light, Paul glided past me into a quiet whirl of snow. I saw then his command and skill, his strength and grace, that would power him up the Mountain.

And what I would not part with I have kept.[7]

East from Moffat, Colorado, is also the way to the blood of Christ, resurrected and elevated for all to see in the disquieting Sangre de Cristo mountain range. At the base of that jagged chain of fourteen-thousand-foot peaks rests Crestone, home to Lorain, and—as we would soon discover—to ancient world religions and many youthful ones as well.

At Moffat we swapped the road map for Lorain's elaborate written directions. Although it was past midnight we were awake and attentive, suspecting that successful navigation to Lorain's home was the first trial she had set for us—a qualifying exam of sorts to earn our seats in her class. In a dark landscape perforated by bouncing headlights, we searched for the designated landmarks—old gates, rock outcrops, basins, cottonwood trees, dirt roads with no apparent names—natural signs that would guide us to our destination.

We passed the test. Quietly we emerged from our car and opened the outside door to the downstairs guest room, not wanting to wake Lorain. As we entered the dark room, however, we heard a mysterious, rhythmic sound overhead. The chanting of contemplative exercises, the steady beat of the shaman's drum, the incantations of a native tongue? No—the drone of a television. As it turned out, Lorain was fast asleep on the upstairs couch, having tried to stay awake for us with the aid of a loud TV.

It makes me wonder. We protect ourselves from wisdom by insisting that it arrive wrapped in ancient robes. Perhaps the very idea of the sage, the spiritual guide, is dangerous. We insist that she be someone outside our community, someone not of our time or place. Yet wisdom may just as likely lie in places or individuals close to home, in almost any person, place, or thing to which we are sufficiently attentive. When we travel to Tibet in search of wisdom, what opportunities for learning do we pass in the thousands of miles on the way? "Why give up your own seat and wander about in the dusty realms of foreign countries?" asked Dogen, the thirteenth-century Zen monk.[8]

Dogen knew all about the value of staying put. He taught that our greatest aim, enlightenment, is achieved by *sitting*. And of course when we stand up and walk about and look around, the opportunities for enlightenment don't stop. Consider the openings near home and work—the backyard oak tree, the laying hen, the powerlines, the deserted lot, the earsplitting neighbor, the carefree child, the carrot on the cutting board, the curious student, the *books*—and let's not forget our inward musings (as Emerson noted, "A man should learn to detect and watch that gleam of light which flashes across his mind from within, more than the luster of the firmament of bards and sages").[9] How much do we neglect, daily? There is an eternity's worth to explore within a five-minute walk or a single moment of unbroken attention.

"I have traveled a good deal in Concord," Thoreau professed with gentle irony. Could I say as much about my home in Poughkeepsie? An eighteenth-century vicar, William Gilpin, recommended that if we are to experience truly the landscape close to home, we should imagine that we are lost and are the first to set foot there. I am well familiar with this technique. But can we not discover the world anew while acknowledging its familiarity? Can we not be in the company of others? Why must our most fruitful journeys be solitary and exotic? Do we travel to distant places because here at home we are blinded by what Percy Shelley called "the veil of familiarity"?[10] Do we assume that there is nothing new to see or learn in the familiar? There are some, such as Martin Buber, who insist that revelation is most likely to occur in the everyday.

A question, then, might be, *How to remove the veil and see afresh?* Travel is one way. I certainly don't wish to disparage the benefits of travel. That great stay-at-home philosopher, Thoreau, understood as much: "to travel and 'descry new lands' is to think new thoughts, and have new imaginings."[11] Having traveled, we can return home with new sight, behold the familiar in a novel way. In this sense travel can be one-way, for the return can, in fact, lead back to a different home. To newness. To change of heart. To being born again (and again and again and again).

Is this what brought me to Crestone, Colorado? Did I leave my home so I could return reformed? Puberty rites often require of the initiate some kind of solitary travel, and then, if successful, a change of social role at home. On these solitary journeys—whether adrift on a raft or alone on a mountaintop—we seek insight, sources of strength, and a sense of purpose and belonging. After appropriate instruction, we leave the community to return to it, altered. We come of age.

Is my journey to the Southwest, then, a puberty rite? Is it adolescent? Yet why should we think such a passage is needed only at an early age and only once in life? Maturation is surely an ongoing process with many transitions, some perfectly predictable, some devastatingly surprising. Leg hair is inevitable; marital infidelity is not. In this case the difference between the foretold and the unexpected is not a matter of statistics but of revelation. A dramatic discovery as much as a rush of hormones can bring about a profound change in a life. It's quite considerate, I think, that some cultures offer their adolescents prescribed rites to assist their transition. What is my culture offering me as I undergo my passage? A dying marriage, whether the demise be fast or slow, is an experience of death. And at this point in my dying, rebirth seemed hardly reachable.

On my Southwest trip, I sought some of that insight and strength that is supposed to show up as we travel through calamity. Reason, risk, and hope had conspired to lead me to a new place with a friend.

Days Two to Four

Three-Day Workshop with Lorain Fox Davis

In the early morning we woke to a chill in the air and fresh snow on the ground. Mid-June in Crestone. Before venturing upstairs to meet our host and teacher, Paul and I explored—independently—our surroundings. It was hard to do otherwise. In Lorain's house of glass, the outdoor grandeur overwhelms even indoor guests. To the west, north, and east, we were bounded by a horseshoe of huge blue and white mountains. To walk out the front door was to enter a Bierstadt western landscape—vast, raw, and uncluttered.

To the south—the source of wind, commerce, and past invaders—the flat sheet of the Colorado plateau stretches dustily into New Mexico and beyond.

To the east—the source of tales of massacre and snow-capped mountains bloody at sunrise—the high peaks of the Sangre de Cristo pierce the sky in an immense chain from Poncha Pass to Glorieta Pass.

To the west—the source of gold, silver, and the Rio Grande—float implausibly the San Juan Mountains, rugged, uncivilized, and squatting on an eighth of Colorado.

And to the north—the source of the Strongs' funding that helped to establish most of the spiritual centers in Crestone—the two massive ranges converge, parting the waters of the Arkansas River and the Rio Grande, two of the largest watersheds in the nation.

Cupped on three sides by the mountains, Paul and I stood at eight thousand feet in the largest alpine valley in the world—the ever-expanding San Luis Valley. Responsible for its expansion is the Rio Grande Rift running down its middle, the seam where two tectonic plates drift apart. The Rio Grande fills this tear in the earth with motion and shine. As the Valley stretches to the west and east, it is continually topped with sediment from the eroding mountains that enfold it. These mountains also donate the "hidden waters" to the Valley. Mountain streams pour steadily into the Valley and sink quickly from sight into about thirty thousand feet (or five miles) of eroded mountainside—loose rock, sand, and soil. These hidden waters feed numerous wetlands, ponds, and lakes—oases in the desert. Most of the water is cool, but down in the depths the water heats and wells up in hot springs. Hot and cold commingle in this region, in bubbling water in the wetlands or swirling air in regional inversions, as when the cold air from the mountaintops drops and collides with the warmer air drifting upward from the Valley floor.

The earth, wind, and water collude to bring mystery and awe to the isolated Valley. Some claim that the topography of the Valley—a circle that opens to the south—generates intense spiritual energies. Like an electromagnet, spiritual currents circle the Valley and attract to it a particular variety of iron-constituted residents. Trinity itself almost resided here when, in the 1940s, the War Department considered detonating the nation's first atomic bomb ("The Gadget") here in the San Luis Valley. Here again, life attracts death. Oppenheimer understood as much. When asked why he proposed the code name "Trinity" for the first nuclear weapons test, he wrote: "There is a poem of John Donne, written just before his death, which I know and love. From it a quotation: 'As West and East / In all flat Maps—and I am one—are one, / So death doth touch the Resurrection.'"[12] Happily for the San Luis Valley, Trinity, that "destroyer of the worlds," happened elsewhere—in the Jornada del Muerto Valley of New Mexico. And lo, the would-be grounds of nuclear testing became instead the fields of Coors beer's barley.

If there is anything like an inner sanctuary of this baffling valley, it is Crestone, population one hundred, a place for powerful dreams, feral visions, startling illumination, and broken marriages (perhaps such spiritual intensity can tax interpersonal ties). Although I am skeptical of most metaphysical claims, I have no doubt that individuals from a wide variety of cultures and religions would find Crestone's setting spiritually alluring. Its landscape haunts, startles, disturbs, and astonishes. It works its way into your dreams.

I was only mildly surprised when I recently discovered that Crestone and its valley are the subject of a trilogy of books whose content and approach are adequately synopsized by the title of the second volume: *Enter the Valley: UFOs, Religious Miracles, Cattle Mutilations, and Other Unexplained Phenomena in the San Luis Valley.* The series investigates, among other things, "What are the strange rumbling noises coming from underground?" I suppose it would be disrespectful all around to suggest that those bizarre noises are Lorain's late-night TV broadcasted and transmuted by the Valley's network of underground aquifers. I should read the trilogy before I judge it, especially since it promises to reveal "the story of one of the most bizarre regions on the face of the earth and its chilling implications for the rest of humanity." I wonder what could possibly be more chilling for this valley than to have nearly received the heat of Trinity? One thing is sure: there is nothing chilling about Crestone's Lorain Fox Davis.

When Paul and I finally went upstairs, Lorain greeted us, a gentle-looking five-foot-five Cree and Blackfeet Native American in her mid-fifties. Her face commanded attention and radiated graciousness, liveliness, and intelligence. I may be cheating here—perhaps I didn't actually read so much in her face from our first meeting in her Crestone kitchen. Memories of what turn out to be significant first encounters are often filled in with information subsequently acquired. In a way, these retellings of first encounters must begin where they end; they must confirm and foretell what we now know to be true (hence

Jesus's miraculous birth). So, gracious, wise, and spirited—this is how I remember Lorain as she offered me coffee on that first morning.

During the next three days, we ate well and laughed often. But mostly we worked hard together, exploring Native American notions of contemplation and landscape, unlearning many of the false assumptions Paul and I had brought with us to the Southwest. We discovered that "landscape"—that sublime vista between us and the horizon—is a concept alien to most Native American traditions. This alone was worth the trip. But we learned new, positive lessons as well. Through a combination of lecture, conversation, and contemplative sessions, Lorain patiently guided us in Cree, Blackfeet, and Lakota perspectives on the land and on much else. Although not easily named, the *much else* is what later proved to be most valuable and practical. If I were to disclose the details of our work together—the medicine wheel, the visualizations, the walking meditations, the legends and myths, and the shared personal stories—I would risk betraying a trust. Further, I would be attempting to write a different book, a book about Lorain and her Cree, Blackfeet spirituality. I would be writing of things of which I still know very little. It is more honest to stay with what I do know and can say.

I met Deirdre when I was a visiting instructor at the University of North Carolina at Greensboro. "Visiting Lecturer" is not an especially prestigious title, but I was awed by it. The letter of hire, written by the Chair, concluded with: "Needless to say, we are all very excited about the possibility of your coming to work with us next year." Young and naïve, I never imagined that these words were mere boilerplate. The letter was dated "May 20," my birthday. I kept that letter, suspecting that I would look back at it as being my most significant birthday present. I was not mistaken.

As a child and young teenager, I didn't enjoy school. I spent my time with my friends, talking about silly things—who was mad at whom, who was dating whom—and also occasionally about matters of importance: Why did people love each other? Why did people hate each other? Why was there war? Why poverty? What held the world together? Was there such a thing as Spirit, and if so, did Spirit care about us, about me? In junior high, we discussed these questions around midnight at sleepovers; half an hour later we were sound asleep.

In high school, I tried to avoid reading and writing, and when I had to read or write, I stuck to physics or math—subjects that came easily to me. For the most part, school was not a work of love but a chore. Everything changed when I entered the University of California, Santa Barbara as a physics major. After taking a religious studies course during my first quarter, I changed my major; suddenly, I churned with passionate, intellectual desire.

What happened? That first quarter at Santa Barbara I registered for courses in physics, math, and classical Greek, a natural choice for the grandchild of four Greek immigrants. Finally, I needed a course to satisfy a humanities requirement. A friend told me about an easy, "blow-off" course, "The Religious Dimension." As it turned out, the course was difficult, the instructor uninspiring, the students half-asleep, and the lecturers seen and heard via the thirty TV monitors suspended from the ceiling of the enormous auditorium. Yet the course changed my life. On its reading list I encountered one of the most important books I would ever read: *The Varieties of Religious Experience* by William James, the famous American psychologist and philosopher.

I spent over one hundred hours reading that book, wrestling with each paragraph, endlessly looking up words in the dictionary and concepts and thinkers in the eight-volume *Encyclopedia of Philosophy*. The ideas, the vocabulary, the approach, and the questions were all entirely new to me. James was fascinating: here was a person who *thought*, who invented new ways to see and understand his world. Sometimes, if we are lucky, we meet a person who makes us think: now, here in front of me is a distinct character, someone who stands for something, is grounded in something, hopes and strives for something.

For the first time in my life, I met such a presence in a book, and the book, in turn, introduced me to a new world in which ideas, concepts, arguments, books, and conversation were pearls of immeasurable worth. James wrote intelligently about life—the art and work of becoming more fully human. And he wrote about religion—its greatness and its folly. The same questions my young friends and I had grappled with in our own untutored way were skillfully and carefully addressed by James.

That he called himself both a scientist and a philosopher made him all the more attractive to me, given that I self-identified as a natural scientist. I was intrigued by his project of developing a "science of religion." I fell in love—with James, yes, but also with books, with thoughtful questions and compelling arguments, with the university and the humanities, with a world where people devoted their lives to exploring the messy and ambiguous tangles of experience.

My newfound intellectual appetite led me to novels, philosophy, plays, psychology, children's stories, religion, music, history, film, anthropology, and art. The university opened its myriad doors to my essentially uneducated mind. During the week, I read assigned texts, wrote papers, studied for exams, and met with faculty. I spent Friday and Saturday nights on the seventh floor of Davidson Library, roving among the language and literature holdings, reading novels and plays that I pulled at random from the shelves. At the time, UCSB had a world-class faculty but a largely uncompetitive student body; nearly every student applicant was admitted and many were not highly invested in their studies. The professors welcomed me. I was starved for knowledge, they for motivated students. They were all mine.

About halfway through my freshman year, I took a walk with

an "older woman"—Alice Bartle, a senior majoring in drama. As we circled the campus lagoon at sunset, she asked, "Mark, what are your plans for later on?" I was glad she asked. "I'm going to change my major from physics to religious studies; then, after four years of philosophy and religion at UCSB, I'm going to divinity school for three years for a master's degree, learning from people who actually *believe* in religion. After that, I'll get my PhD at a secular university and bring together theological and religious studies." Alice laughed. "I was asking about your *dinner* plans," she said.

Alice had good reason to laugh. Here I was, eighteen years old and plotting the next fourteen years of my life. As a senior, Alice dismissed my long-term plans, assuring me that after four years at UCSB, I would be eager to escape university life.

I never attempted an escape. I never, as they say, "took time off." Time off from what? My heart's desire? After I graduated from UCSB, I studied at Princeton Theological Seminary for three years, earned my master's degree, and then moved across the street to Princeton University to pursue doctoral studies in a secular religious studies program. The plan I had laid out for Alice Bartle could not have been more accurate. But it was not commitment to my plan that kept me on that academic path. Nor was it the dream of an academic job, a professional destination at the end of it all. Don't get me wrong: a professorship would have been a dream come true. But during most of my graduate education, I wasn't thinking about the future. I was being borne along by a love, by a desire to read and write, to ponder and wonder—and to mature in these endeavors. The pursuit of knowledge had become my true home.

In the afternoon of our second day with Lorain Fox Davis, we went on a field trip regarding—or offering regards to—the gods of the Crestone Valley. Within a five-mile radius, Paul, Lorain, and I visited no fewer than nine significant religious sites: the Crestone Mountain Zen Center; the Tashi Gomang, a Buddhist stupa and study center; the Haidakhandi Center, a Hindu temple and ashram; the Spiritual Life Institute, a Carmelite monastery; the Bhutanese Tibetan Retreat Center; the Savitri House, a retreat facility dedicated to the spiritual vision of Sri Aurobindo; the Little Shepherd in the Hills Episcopal Church, the oldest non-Native spiritual center in Crestone, built in 1885 and dedicated to the fourteenth-century mystic, Julian of Norwich; the Samten Ling Retreat Center, a Buddhist long-term retreat facility whose name means "the meditation place of the fearless great expanse"; and finally the Sanctuary House, a large interreligious worship center with eight prayer rooms, representing diverse traditions, ringed around an exact replica of the eleven-tiered labyrinth found at the Chartres Cathedral.

When we arrived at the Sanctuary House, the Sufi-Christian director was in the process of moving large rocks in the construction of the labyrinth. Beside him, sinuous wooden forms held wet concrete in curved paths. The director and his assistant, hard at work on this labyrinth in the middle of the desert, seemed to find nothing more natural than the construction of a huge religious center in a tiny settlement on a vast plain.

We didn't have time that afternoon to visit the Vajra Vidya Retreat Center, the Sacred Mountains Foundation, the Sage House, the Full Circle Foundation for Conscious Health, the Yeshe Khorlo Center, or the Yeshe Rangsal Retreat Land—to name but a few more of the spiritual centers in and around Crestone. Everyone we met on that cold bright June afternoon seemed to me a person with a mission, with a calling. They were not fanatics. They did not proselytize or speak in strange tongues. Yet all were clearly committed to a way of life that entailed something more than advancing a career, caring for a family, or pursuing pleasure. Their way was spiritual but not otherworldly. For example, their religious sites comprised organic farms, passive solar greenhouses, photovoltaic panels, and much else that suggested a dedication to environmental sustainability. Some consider small-town Crestone to be the nation's alternative building capital, given the number of homes and structures made of such materials as straw bales, volcanic rock, old tires, and soda cans. An alternative, sustainable life, I suppose, is an apt description of these people's shared aspiration—where work and play are balanced and integrated; where the line between co-worker and friend is permeable; where time is placed before money; where community, food, and land are thoughtfully linked; and where distinctions between religious and secular life are blunted, for it is understood that all good work is sacred, whether it be moving a rock or writing a hymn.

It's unwise, I realize, to indulge in sentimental descriptions of communities, families, and places I barely know. Coming in from the bright outdoors, eyes need time to adjust to see the shadows. We risk discontent with our own homes when we gaze on those of others from the outside alone. I have already alluded to the many broken marriages in Crestone. I can easily imagine the sundry human pathologies that might prosper in this Eden's soil: small-town gossip, sexual affairs, competition for wealthy donors and spiritual standing—the customary mix of sex, money, and power. Still, I was impressed with Crestone's kooky inhabitants. I can't help but believe that, despite the human hardships that trouble all communities, those residents of Crestone sustain themselves through an approach to life more graceful than my own.

While visiting the Lindisfarne Chapel at the Mountain Zen Center, a young woman dressed in jeans and a tank top asked, "What brought *you* here?" I explained that Paul and I were professors who had traveled to the Southwest to study with two Native American teachers and learn about their philosophical, religious, and aesthetic approaches to the land. She replied, "Professors, eh? Well, then Crestone is the right place for you. This is where the teachers are taught."

I learned how to teach at the University of North Carolina at Greensboro. When I first arrived at Foust Hall, the stately building that housed the religious studies department, I was the lowliest of the several "visiting" and "adjunct" faculty—and the only one without a doctorate. Having studied in my doctoral program only three years, I was essentially a graduate student on loan to UNC-G, yet I walked through Foust's doors confident and optimistic. I felt like I was coming home.

What brought me to Greensboro? Only months before, on a humid July day in Princeton, I came to the sudden conclusion that I should take leave from my graduate program, gain some teaching experience in a temporary academic position, and then return to Princeton to finish my program, where I still had two years of guaranteed funding. Within two months, I had applied for, received, and moved into the temporary position at Greensboro. In light of my status, I should have shown the same—or more—deference to my senior colleagues, Paul Courtright and Henry Levinson, as did my fellow junior colleagues. But at the time I was too excited, too aflame, too gung-ho even to notice such things as rank. I was on an academic high. I was going to become a professor—to read, write, *and* teach—to walk the halls of academia not as a student, but as a teaching member of the ancient *akademeia*, the Academy. And so with much—too much—aplomb and liveliness, I marched in, embraced Courtright and Levinson as kindred souls, and was received with warmth and collegiality. I was young, insensitive, and fiercely resolute.

I had much to learn, and, luckily, much was offered to me by junior and senior colleagues alike. I have written of those moments of chance or grace that help us on our routes through life. My two years at Greensboro were replete with such moments: the students welcomed my enthusiasm and forgave my incompetence as a teacher, even insisting on calling me *Dr.* Cladis, no matter how often I reminded them that I didn't have a doctorate; and my colleagues, within and outside the religious studies department, treated me with respect, generosity, and kindness.

But Greensboro's greatest gifts to me were Paul Courtright and Henry Levinson, those senior colleagues whose wisdom and generosity continue to shape my life. When I think of them and their offerings, I am reminded of Emerson's line, "The benefit overran the merit the first day, and has overran the merit ever since."[13] How to repay such givers? How to show enough gratitude to Courtright—the man who hired me, who taught me about building a department and thinking institutionally, who introduced me to Wild Turkey bourbon and the art of sharing conviviality with colleagues and their families?

And how to repay Henry—the brilliant philosopher of religion, the inspiring teacher, and the benevolent colleague, whose multiple sclerosis, which tormented him even then, would eventually take his life? My first colleague in my field, Henry worked at the intersection of philosophy, religion, and ethics, and had written two dazzling books on none other than William James, the very thinker who had transformed my life ten years before. From Henry, I learned the knack of philosophical conversation over lunch and the role of humor and festivity in scholarly work. Most importantly, I learned how to teach.

W. H. Auden once said, "A professor is someone who talks in someone else's sleep." During my first semester at UNC-G, I was that professor. During a seminar that met in the library, as I was interrogating Evans-Pritchard's ideological biases in his anthropological study of the Nuer people of South Sudan, a blind student stared to snore, loudly. The rest of us were dumbfounded. What was I to do? I let him sleep, dismissed the class, and later that day asked Henry if I could sit in on one of his courses.

I joined Henry's course, History of Philosophy of Religion, and sat in on a lecture on Hegel—not easy for anyone, let alone young undergraduates. But Henry addressed them. He offered them the heart of Hegel and, in the process, his own heart.

With conviction, gracefulness, and love, Henry began:

> Hegel was afraid that the people of his age—of our age—were suffering from a serious disease. It wasn't the sort of disease that could be cured by a doctor—at least not a medical doctor. What the people needed—what we need—is a special kind of therapist: one who thoroughly understands the dis-ease, and knows how to cure people of it. The disease is known as spiritlessness, or alienation, and Hegel himself is the solution.

Henry didn't begin by rehearsing all the various critiques of Hegel or by situating Hegel in his historical context. He started with why Hegel matters, why we should still be reading Hegel today. As so, with the help of Henry, I found the teacher in me. I had needed permission to be myself in the classroom, a facilitator of the kind of learning I myself so loved rather than an imitator of another breed of teacher. Henry gave me license to fling my arms wide open and gather my students to me, engaging them in the exciting and risky act of intellectual discovery, bringing together the ideas of the mind and the passions of the heart.

During our day trip to the religious sites of Crestone, I couldn't stop wondering about the role of the Colorado Plateau and mountains in the development of these rich spiritual communities. Archeological evidence suggests that Native Americans had been traveling to the valley to perform sacred rituals and vision quests thousands of years before the arrival of Mexicans or Europeans. Later, the valley became especially significant to the Ute Native Americans, and many Navajos believe the valley is just below the site of emergence, the *xajiinai*, in the San Juan Mountains.

Is this intense concentration of spirituality in the valley a *response* to a beckoning land? We shape the land around us with bulldozers and irrigators. "Landscaping," we call it. We also shape the land with our conceptions and preconceptions.

These determine what qualifies as picturesque or grotesque, lovely or bleak. This conceptual landscaping is perhaps more profound than physical landscaping, for it governs the track of the bulldozer, the placement of trees and shrubs, the application of pesticides and fertilizers, the height and shape of walls and buildings. After visiting the many religious sites of Crestone, however, I began to think less about landscaping and more about *humanscaping*—that is, about how the land itself shapes its human inhabitants.

To my knowledge, the question of how humans are informed by the land has not been greatly explored. We scholars are accustomed to the view that humans perceive and experience the world through culturally specific, sociolinguistic lenses. I don't doubt that. When we do quarrel with this view, we pose the Nature vs. Nurture question: what's the greater influence on our lives, genetic constitution or social environment? I'm writing now of a third influence: the way external landscape shapes inner identity, character, and the emergent communities of which we are a part. Are we not informed and reformed by the landscapes that enfold us?

Terry Tempest Williams is one of the few writers who approach what I am calling this "third influence." She writes, "There is no defense against an open heart and a supple body in dialogue with wildness. Internal strength is an absorption of the external landscape. We are informed by beauty, raw and sensual. Through an erotics of place our sensitivity becomes our sensibility."[14] Our sensitivity to this empirical world—our openness to being struck by it, shaped by it—informs our sensibility, that is, our interpretive powers, our awareness, our ability to make sense of things. The land surrounding us, then, can inform our aesthetic sensibility and even ethical identity.

Williams writes vividly of the encounter with wildness. Those of us who have experience of the wild can easily conjure our own image of this encounter. Reaching a summit just as the sun sets fiery in the west; noticing the music and play of light in a mountain brook's stony course; walking at dusk through a meadow and meeting a family of deer whose alert, motionless bodies bring our own to rest. Moments in such artless wildness can be transformative, displacing anxiety with calmness, dullness with awareness, despair with joy, arrogance with humility. It can happen. And so living—dwelling—in proximity to wild places can shape us in ways manifold and beneficial.

From what I know of Williams, however, she would not want to confine wildness to "scenic" landscapes alone. In Williams's mind, as in Thoreau's, the wild is not so much a place but a quality or condition that may be found in any place or person. "It is in vain," Thoreau warned, "to dream of a wildness distant from ourselves. There is none such. It is the bog in our brain and bowels, the primitive vigor of Nature in us, that inspires that dream."[15] The wild confronts all things tame, domesticated, or highly controlled and regulated. If we seek to cultivate and manage every inch of the earth, every minute of our lives, we risk becoming the living dead. This is not to say all domestication and cultivation—social conventions, laws, routines, things predictable, and so on—are deadening or bereft of wildness. A customary Tuesday lunch meeting can invite wildness just as a garden can. If the cultivated is not to turn stultifying, it will depend on its dialogue with the wild. In different ways, both Thoreau and Williams present a spiritual solution to the human problem of over-management of the wild, otherwise known as hubris. Both authors ask that we invite the wild into our lives. "In Wildness is the preservation of the world."[16]

Wildness, then, cannot be understood exclusively as scenic wilderness. At the mall, in the housing development, and in the tenements of New York City—like sunshine, the wild suffuses the urban and suburban, too. And if unpredictability is what, in part, defines the wild, then it is found in AIDS clinics and cancer wards. The wild breathes life and also death. Sometimes its opportunities for growth are our final ones. Death, in these cases, becomes our last instructor in wildness. The journey to death can strip away pretense and grant a transformed sense of life, a sense of wild that may teach the healthy something about the art of living.

"Tell me the landscape in which you live," wrote Ortega y Gasset, "and I will tell you who you are." Death and despair are landscapes of sorts. "Tell me the suffering you have seen," we might say, "and I will tell you who you are."

At UNC-G, after years of Platonic love—the *eros* of books and friends—I longed for a different kind of love. I had casually mentioned this longing to Cathy Levinson, Henry's wife, and she suggested that I "get out there." Those words terrified me. What did "getting out there" entail? Buying a new shirt, joining a gym, roaming bars for a lifelong partner? What about a personal ad? *Single guy in late 20s seeks nerdy woman for company after library hours.*

As much as I flinched at Cathy's suggestion, it was her encouragement that caused me to ask Deirdre out to a date. When I first saw her, Deirdre was standing beside an academic poster at a graduate student biology conference. Although "mechanisms of intracellular protein transport" is a fascinating topic, I was more interested in the presenter than the presentation. I had been looking for a face that would make me whole. Deirdre's looked promising.

What did I see in her face? What in it compelled me to ask her for a date and eventually for her hand in marriage? Did her face speak to a bright, agile mind matched by intense introspection and stillness? Or a way and manner entirely soothing, supportive, warm, even cozy? A motion unhurried, yet purposeful? Yes, all that and more. That pretty face—with its emerald eyes, full lips, long ginger-red hair, and a recurrent pensive, even plaintive, expression—intrigued and attracted me.

When I first approached her and asked about her biology project, Deirdre's eyes would not meet mine. I persisted with questions, and finally, as if yielding to the inevitable, her eyes lifted and piercingly held mine. My confidence suddenly faltered. I found myself speechless. During that silence between us, her left hand fiddled with a colorful key chain. That chain held a key that would soon be powerless to unlock a door, an event that would propel Deirdre into my life. The key would also explain a small blemish on the left side of her face. But all that would come later.

There had been times as a graduate student when I was acutely lonely. I can recollect specific episodes of despair—home on break, sitting in the quiet Stanford Memorial Chapel; Princeton in the summer, walking alone along Carnegie Lake; my tiny Greensboro apartment, on my knees in desperate prayer. I was longing for *that* face—the face of love.

Freudians might call this a regression, a neurotic longing for some elemental motherly gaze. Yet why should we let go of our longing for such a face? Do we not first discover our own face in the faces of our first loves? Do we not again and again rediscover who we are in the presence of love? Can desire for love not be understood as part of a journey toward that Source which subsumes both romantic and parental love?

In the *Symposium*, Plato's dramatic dialogue on love, Aristophanes tells his drinking buddies a wry story about the origin of love. In his story, the first human individuals comprised two halves, essentially two people who fit perfectly together to form a sphere, from which four arms and four legs protruded like a spider's. When these early ball-shaped humans became too arrogant, Zeus thrust a lightning bolt down their centers, splitting each circle person into two incomplete humans, whom he then scattered around the globe. Although Aristophanes was a comic poet, there is nothing droll about his closing lines on love. "We human beings will never attain happiness unless we find perfect love, unless we each come across the love of our lives and thereby recover our original nature."[17] Here Aristophanes names the human plight, task, and hope—to find "perfect love." Love, in his view, is the longing to be made whole.

When Deirdre and I married, about six months after I first saw her, I believed that my longing and loneliness would disappear. I believed that the subtle, sometimes intense, sadness that clung to my work and life would vanish. That's a lot of pressure to put on a relationship. Though I did not see it then, a darkness hovered over my marriage, a darkness under which neither of us would ever be made whole.

All landscapes shape us—those within and without, those of grief and love, and those of steel and streams. I don't pretend to know which environments are most favorable to human flourishing, nor can I begin to name the range of subtle strokes by which they chisel us. Still I suspect there are particular places with special character and power to shape and mold us. I wonder, are there intrinsic, physical characteristics of Crestone and its valley that have attracted and shaped its visionaries? Or are its visionaries responsible for creating and shaping Crestone, projecting on its landscape something held within themselves? We may say that certain people are particularly open to the influence of particular sites, even as they bring to such sites a particular moral and aesthetic imagination. But the question remains: Is there such a thing as an *intrinsically* extraordinary site?

If there are intrinsically extraordinary sites for human visitation or dwelling, I'd like to think that there are enough of them to provide everyone—all of us—with access. According to the Cree, we are never more than one hundred miles from a powerful, sacred site. An even more egalitarian view is found in Thich Nhat Hanh. "This spot where you sit," he assures us, "is your own spot. It is on this very spot and in this very moment that you can become enlightened. You don't have to sit beneath a special tree in a distant land."[18]

If this is correct, then in the spiritual realm as in the political, individual rights are rarely fully exercised and we fail to avail ourselves of the opportunities offered to us. There are no extraordinary sites. Every place, Thich Nhat Hanh seems to say, offers the same opportunity to gain knowledge and freedom. Everything we need to learn we can learn anywhere, if we ask the right question of a grain of wheat, a ray of sun, a stab of pain, a face of love. Anywhere will do.

So which is it? Do distinct landscapes shape us in distinct ways, or will any place do? Do we need Shiprock and Crestone? Let me begin with what I know—with the basics.

One. Some sites are not intrinsically exceptional, but rather become significant by way of cultural stories and traditions. A while ago I visited St. Catherine's monastery on Jordan's Sinai Peninsula. I knew that St. Catherine's was built at the foot of Mount Sinai and I had expected that I would immediately recognize the mountain. Even if it were not shrouded mysteriously in clouds or illuminated by numinous light, surely the height, breadth, or shape of Mount Sinai would distinguish it. But distinguished it wasn't. I had to ask, "On which of these plain rocky crags did Moses meet God?" Tradition anointed that indistinct mountaintop with infinite distinction.

Two. Some landscapes, like that of Shiprock or Crestone, are spectacular by almost any standard. To deny this would be to cling irrationally to the philosophical theory that *all* perception is subjective cultural projection. Common sense tells me otherwise. Show me a Shiprock, and I'll show you a monument.

Three. Impressive sites such as Shiprock or Crestone attract to them cultural production, like magnets for the social filings of myths, songs, stories, and rituals. These in turn infuse the features of the landscape with rich, interpretive traditions, making these places all the more significant.

Four. These impressive sites, fashioned in the past by some combination of geology and culture, can shape their current inhabitants. Their inhabitants, in turn, contribute to the landscape, adding their own stories, participating in the ancient echo between people and place.

Five. In shaping us, a place potentially contributes to our maturation as human beings. Given the proper attention, a place can tutor our emotions, develop our character, and expand our reasoning. It can endow a particular path on which we may travel through life.

Six. Although different land imparts different lessons, all instances of "humanscaping" share this: they enable us to become more alert and aware. The external landscape inspires consideration of an oft-neglected interior landscape. As we look outward with care and attention, the land reflects back our focus, inwardly, instructively. The land acts as a mirror—there, even, in the dark wet bark and pale green leaves, or in the dry ochre sand and brittle creosote brush—except that it reveals not our outward image but an internal one. Having traveled inward, our focus—now sharper—may return to the outward world, changed and educated. The land becomes our teacher, a conductor of the voyage, moving concurrently inward and outward, toward knowledge of self and knowledge of world.

Anywhere, then, will do. But not everywhere. To learn from the land and to see ourselves in and through it, we need to rest somewhere. All lessons require time. Teachers and students must remain together in the same place long enough to trust, communicate with, and teach each other. Instruction from the land, too, requires some steadfastness to a place.

Seven. Here I take the most untried step and reach an unexplored region, a *terra incognita.* After we have learned deeply from a place, we both remain there and move beyond it. This is what Wittgenstein said of the one who works his way through the propositions in the *Tractatus*: "He must, so to speak, throw away the ladder after he has climbed up it." Although the land, unlike a book of logical atomism, is never dispensable and certainly not disposable, the lessons of the land point ultimately to something beyond the land, the way the motherly gaze points toward an ultimate love. Yet what is beyond I cannot name, and I am reminded of Wittgenstein's final remark in the *Tractatus*: "What we can't speak about we must pass over in silence."[19]

❧

After our first date, I kissed Deirdre on the cheek, intimated that I'd like to see her again, and said goodnight. It was midnight. About thirty minutes later, I was surprised by a knock on my apartment door. I opened the door and saw Deirdre, clutching her backpack. She asked if she could spend the night.

Her roommates had changed the locks, "probably," she suggested, because her "physically abusive ex-boyfriend had recently made a scene there." Recent ex-boyfriend? Physically abusive? Locked out by roommates? It was a lot to take in. Naturally, I invited her in.

My approach to love and sex had always been slow and patient. Normally, I would have dated Deirdre for about two or even three months before sleeping with her. But the woman of my dreams was asking to spend the night, and at half past midnight, I surrendered my measured approach. Deirdre and I had moved in together.

Of course, now I see things for what they were. I longed for a companion to erase my loneliness and to support emotionally my pursuit of all things academic. She needed a place to stay and an escape from an abusive relationship. Perhaps I should have known better. But we were, after all, in love. I suppose at the time I idealized her. We find our lovers as much as we *make* them. And Deirdre offered much to idealize: she was smart but not pedantic; utterly agreeable but not a pushover; quiet but not aloof; beautiful but not beautified or primped.

Still, I knew that ours was not the ideal way to start a relationship, and after living together for a couple of months, I suggested she move out—not because things were going poorly, but because I wanted us to build a strong foundation while living independently. She agreed, and we explored some options. For Deirdre, however, moving out was logistically and financially more difficult than staying. And so we submitted to the beauty of our sudden togetherness—rejecting, in the process, the more sensible alternative.

Edmund Burke noted that beauty, that ineluctable precursor of love, is "no creature of our reason." We surrender to beauty, embrace its disorienting charm, and jettison our dependable compass. I do not want to become suspicious of beauty, its senseless wonder, its propulsion toward a particular person, place, or thing. I still believe in beauty. Yet I know also that beauty sometimes fails us, as it did Deirdre and me. Looking back now with the rationality I lacked then, I understand ours was a marriage of textbook co-dependency between workhorse husband and taciturn wife. She made few demands, provided emotional comfort, and allowed me to dedicate myself to my books. I reciprocated in kind, enabling her to pursue her quiet, introverted private life. She didn't need to work, and I didn't need to stop working.

It was dark when Lorain, Paul, and I returned, exhausted, from our field trip to the religious sites of Crestone. The next morning we enjoyed a final ritual together, and then Paul and I offered Lorain gifts. I gave her honey from my backyard bees; Paul gave her an indigenous Australian message stone. Each gift stood for a feature of our internal-external landscape, a landscape challenged and enhanced by the gifts Lorain had given us. After a final farewell, Paul and I departed in our rental car, passing through the land in silence.

Days Five to Seven

Arrival at the two-day workshop with Ben Barney at Lukachukai in the Navajo Nation

Yes, "arrival by noon at Lukachukai"—this is what our itinerary stated. Here's what it *didn't* state.

On day five, Paul and I drove to Farmington, New Mexico. The next morning, after a brief visit to Shiprock, we drove southwest toward Lukachukai and soon came upon a crossroad. We could take the smooth, wide, paved highway north to Teec Nos Pos, west to Mexican Water, and then back south to Lukachukai—not a direct route, to be sure (more like driving around an immense horseshoe), but a dependable one. Alternatively, we could take the proverbial shortcut: a narrow dirt road cutting directly west to Lukachukai over the Chuska mountains.

As we approached the crossroads, discussing our options, we saw to our right a Navajo family getting into a pickup truck. Eager for advice from some locals, we asked about the condition of the dirt mountain pass, whose road sign claimed it was washed out and closed. The driver, about to climb into her pickup, turned and looked impassively at me, then Paul, then our rented coupe. After a pause, she responded, "The road's pretty bad." At the time, we knew something of Navajo understatement, but evidently not enough. We took the Chuska pass.

There are shortcuts that we insist on taking, no matter the price of such parsimony. Imagine us, driving two miles per hour in constant fear of a rock bursting our oil pan or a gaping pothole trapping a tire. As with many ill-advised journeys, our path began smoothly and without offense—that is, until we reached the summit. Toss a frog in boiling water and it will leap for safety. Place the same frog in a kettle of cool water, bring to a slow boil, and get frog legs. As gradually as a slow simmer, our road, bit by bit, stone by stone, lured us into peril.

In Greensboro, I wrote lectures endlessly for my three new courses each semester. On most evenings, I would pore over the hundreds of pages that I had assigned to my students and try to produce original, engaging presentations. The work was exhausting—equivalent to writing a couple of academic papers each day. Before Deirdre, this was often a lonesome toil, especially when performed late at night. But with her, it was now less taxing. I could push myself hard, delight in my academic loves, and not fear a fall into despondence or painful solitude. Ours was an entirely gentle relationship; we talked little, sharing meals and passing time in warm, protracted silence. We rarely argued.

About five years into our marriage, I admitted to myself that Deirdre was, by nature, utterly retiring and shy—that our union would never brim with impassioned conversation or household bickering or belly laughter. Yet, at night, we held on to each other tightly, as if clinging to a lifesaver. In the morning we would part ways, carrying with us our shared comfort and dependency. There was much to be grateful for, and at the time, I was grateful. I felt blessed by Deirdre and offered thanksgiving. Yet the comfort of our relationship, I realize now, did not offer *life*. Later in our marriage, when we were living in Poughkeepsie, I would sometimes find myself repeating the refrain, *Life, life, life*. It was a plea for something more than contentment. Still, I believed that the marriage was good enough. It was the path I had chosen, years earlier when we had only known each other for a few months.

I remember it well. We went on a two-week road trip early in our courtship from San Francisco to Portland, Oregon. That's plenty of days to travel those six hundred miles. There was something contemplative about that road trip that perhaps characterized our relationship as well. We drove slowly, stopped frequently, talked minimally, and caressed constantly. New Age music—the piano of George Winston and the guitar of Alex De Grassi—suffused our car and lives. Above Lake Tahoe, hiking on a quiet trail, Deidre came upon some tightly curled, emerging young ferns. With childlike wonder and utter delight, she gazed at them for at least half an hour. And as I watched Deirdre watching the ferns, their fiddleheads like tiny, fisted hands, I knew I was in love. After six months together, we were married.

In a small Appalachian town, in a small Episcopal church, we walked down the aisle flanked by thirty guests. The priest was pleasant, but a stranger to us. The food at the reception was satisfactory—mostly homemade sandwiches cut in small, bite-sized squares, assorted fruit, and a white sheet cake with vanilla frosting. The town was "dry," so for drinks we served iced tea and lemonade. But none of this mattered. I was getting married. I was settling down. And my wife was bright and attractive, tender, and entirely good-natured. She understood me, and I her, though her emerald eyes were often shadowed with mystery or sorrow.

Those eyes were puffy on the wedding day. The night before, at the rehearsal dinner, she had cried much during and after the "toasts." I had thought hers were tears of joy, but as I later learned, they were tears of quiet anger. During the toasts, my family members and friends shared stories and memories that honored me, while hers, she felt, told stories that belittled her, even suggesting that I was her rescuer.

Sad recollection! Her unhappiness, her anger and passiveness that magnified each other, her hatred of the savior trope. And who could blame her? But while I was sympathetic, it was not the celebration I had hoped for. On the night before a wedding, do we not imagine signs of future hope and joy? At the time, I did try to focus on joy—after all, my bride was the image of gentleness and care. In retrospect, I see omens of discord and despair.

We honeymooned in the Appalachian mountains of North Carolina. The weeklong stay in an isolated, modest mountain home matched the tenor of our courtship and foretold the tenor of our marriage. We read. We cooked. We built fires. We held each other. Quietude and tenderness, like the warmth from the stove, permeated our days. That was in late December. By New Year's Day, I had returned alone to Greensboro to begin my dissertation. When Deirdre joined me two weeks later, I had outlined the entire dissertation and written the first chapter. Within four months, while teaching full-time, I completed the dissertation. The marriage, one might say, was working well.

In North Carolina, I met my first colleagues, taught my first courses, met my first wife. My adult life had begun smoothly. But I was headed, in slow motion, into peril, and I never saw it coming.

First there were the bumps. As Paul and I headed over the Chuska pass, I slowed appropriately and dodged what I could. Next came the craters, first as wide as tires, then wider and deeper as we drove. Finally, we came upon large rocks—small boulders, really—standing in our way like wartime barricades. The bumps, craters, and rocks often worked together to cause us to stop or even reverse our course to attempt another tack. I was driving, but Paul was equally piloting. For hours we plotted and conferred, every five or six feet, about the way forward, while the earth and stone grazed and clawed the undercarriage of our car.

At one point, when the way forward *and* backward seemed hopeless, I reminded Paul that I had declined the supplemental rental auto insurance. If we had a cell phone, we wondered, could we call Budget Rental and request the additional insurance en route? "Yes, we initially declined it," we would explain, "but we're having second thoughts…. Why have we changed our minds, you ask? Well, it recently occurred to us that given the vicissitudes of life, the vulnerability of a car's oil pan, and the transactional relation between the two, extra insurance seems like a good idea." That was the call we imagined, and within five minutes we saw our fears realized—but in someone else's car.

I think it was a blue Nova or some other discontinued model, its hood up and its young Navajo owner peering up from below at its underbelly. We asked the unfortunate driver if he needed help, though it wasn't clear what we, the philosopher and poet, had to offer (words of hope?). He walked over to our car, smiled, and inquired pleasantly, "Have a *rubber* oil pan?" Humor in a tight spot is often the Navajo way. Panic is closer to my own.

Thirty minutes later the road gradually tamed and evened out. Just where the dirt road began to merge into a paved federal highway, we saw an orange highway sign warning: BUMP. "Bump!" we cried in fear, but the jolt was almost imperceptible. We had traveled from Navajo understatement to bureaucratic overstatement. Imagine the signs if the Highway Department had placed them higher up the mountain pass. CHASM. BOULDER. ABYSMAL TRENCH.

I have a photograph of Paul and me standing next to that orange "bump" sign. It sits on my desk in my study and reminds me each morning that my daily digital planner—my scrupulous itinerary—provides only a faint prediction of my day. Life's greatest bumps seldom come with warnings—and if they do, we often disregard them.

Like the Chuska pass, our arrival to the Navajo Nation came with considerable warning. Whether the warning was for our benefit or that of the Navajos I will never know, but its reality was unquestionable. After crossing into Lukachukai, home to Ben Barney and the Diné College where he teaches, we drove to the Thriftway gas station and convenience store, where Ben would meet us at noon. We parked in the back and made our way exhaustedly around the station toward the entrance. About twenty feet from the door, I pointed out a small twister in the distance. "A dust devil," Paul observed, "what the Australians call a willy-willy." As we watched idly, the dust devil gathered in both size and speed. Before long, it was across the street, pausing as if spinning its wheels, and then suddenly crossing the street and violently shaking a pickup truck a few yards in front of us.

At about this time it dawned on Paul and me that the dust devil was coming directly for us. We began walking toward the Thriftway entrance, quickening our pace and finally breaking into a sprint as the dust rushed upon us. Once inside the store's entrance, with the twister at our heels, we were unable to close the door. There was something of an explosion as an outside trashcan erupted, spewing paper, dirt, bottles, and cans in every direction, inside and outside, and the dust—it was everywhere.

When it finally settled and our eyes cleared, we met the firm gazes of the two Navajo women behind the counter. Their eyes seemed to hold both amusement and disdain. Here we were, two white guys chased into their store by a cloud of dust and garbage. Items, blown off the shelves, littered the floor along with the dirt and debris; the door hung askance on its hinges; the front of the station looked like a dump site.

When Ben Barney arrived, Paul and I were waiting sheepishly in the shade of the parking lot where we could do little harm. Ben was dressed casually in jeans, an orange T-shirt, and new sneakers. I wished I was meeting him under better circumstances. Yet he acted as if it were only natural to find us behind the Thriftway, outside in the heat on a concrete parking block littered with debris. I knew from Paul that Ben had been a dancer, but his physique was not what I'd expected—hardly slender and graceful, Ben looked more like a muscled, stout construction worker. His height was medium at best, but his stature was commanding. Perhaps his authoritative presence stemmed from his penetrating, almond-shaped eyes, which were set deeply in his olive face and framed by messy gray-streaked black hair. However imposing, Ben flashed a broad, infectious smile and greeted us in Navajo, *yá'át'ééh.*

When we told Ben about the dust devil's destruction, he shook his head slowly and said, "Not a good sign." He went inside the Thriftway without us, and through the window we saw the Navajo women, shaking their heads now, explaining what had taken place. Their conversation was not difficult to imagine.

We've told you, Ben, these white friends of yours come and cause trouble.

Yes, I know, but what could I do? They called and asked if they could visit.

In no uncertain terms, the land had let us know that we did not belong there. I am not suggesting that we should have stayed home instead of visiting the Navajo Nation. But we had received a forceful reminder that we were short-term visitors in a foreign land, and we should not feel at home. The dust devil was a sober counterbalance to Lorain Fox Davis's generous ecumenical spirit. In her company, Paul and I might have been tempted to think that we could somehow become Native. We might have come to believe, at some level, that we had earned the spiritual right to travel self-assuredly among Native Americans, regardless of tribe or place. Yet within five minutes of our arrival in the Navajo Nation, we were quickly—and categorically—set straight.

We often long to fit in where we do not in fact belong. The poet Mary Oliver once yearned to "Enter the Kingdom" of the crows. Her goal seemed modest enough. She did not want to *become* a crow, only to enter their world, to become imperceptible and

> To learn something by being nothing
> A little while but the rich
> Lens of attention.

Yet even this dream is immodest, and the poet knows it.

"The Crows see me," she declares in the first line of the poem. And so we are not surprised to learn by the end that

> ...the crows puff their feathers and cry
> Between me and the sun,
> And I should go now.
> They know me for what I am.
> No dreamer,
> No eater of leaves.[20]

Know me for what I am. This is sometimes our greatest hope, other times our greatest fear. We long for loved ones to know us for who we are. Yet we also hold our breath, praying that our lovers and friends still find us worthy of love after discovering who, in fact, we are—after having revealed our fears, wounds, weaknesses, beliefs, and struggles to believe. We want to be known and to continue to belong—firmly and without question. But there are places and people where and with whom we don't belong, precisely *because* they know us for what we are. In these cases, it is wise to recognize, "I should go now. They know me for what I am." Learn, as Rilke said, to get ahead of all departures.

When to leave a marriage? When to exit a job? I am better at arrivals than departures.

My one-year position at Greensboro was extended to two years, and in that second year—the year of my marriage—I was offered a two-year visiting assistant professor job at Stanford. It was a joint appointment in the philosophy and religious studies departments, surely one of the best job openings of the year. More importantly, my parents lived about a mile from Stanford's main quad in Palo Alto. Five years earlier, I had made the painful decision not to move near my family, turning down a generous offer from Stanford's doctoral program. Now was my chance to return home and live near my elderly parents, at least for a couple of years. In response to Stanford's job offer,

UNC-G's dean offered me a three-year contract and a vague prediction—not a promise—that it would eventually become a tenure-track position. I went with Stanford.

To get ahead of all departures. I suppose that's what I did in this case, but it was not painless. I was leaving Henry. I was leaving the place that had known me for what I was—young, eager, inexperienced—and still embraced me. What if I had stayed? Paul Courtright headed to Emory the year after I went to Stanford. Henry died. And my marriage? Would it have died in Greensboro?

Lost tourists who accidentally wander into the wrong part of town may hope to be inconspicuous—nothing but lenses of attention—when in fact they are unmistakably known as vacationers, often disoriented, with extra cash and limited knowledge of their environment. Stealthily though we may creep into the woods, the land and its wild inhabitants hear us approach as loudly as the early morning garbage truck. To journey incognito ultimately requires that we shed our skin and disappear. But that is not a human option—not, at least, until the end of our lives.

There is nothing wrong with the desire to fit in—on the streets of Rome, in the woods of crows, or in the land of the Navajo. Nothing at all. But acceptance must never be insisted upon. Even with a lifetime of patience, it still may never happen.

I suspect that our idealization of those foreign places rich in beauty, tradition, or culture springs from an elemental need to belong somewhere. The foreign place is often made attractive by the love and care of those who, for generations, have belonged there. If we can figure out where our home is—or more likely, accept where our home is—perhaps we can participate in the good work of building a Rome or a Navajo Nation, of making our own place worthy of visits from others.

Ben Barney is at home in a Rome of sorts. He is to the land of the Navajo what the Victory of Samothrace is to its Greek marble: material and form—body and soul—become one. Like the character of the land he perfectly matches, Ben is open, exacting, unadorned, and relentlessly honest.

I can't help but think that Ben's strong, deep-rooted, no-nonsense character was shaped by a terrain that demands respect, attentiveness, and endurance of its extremities—its heat and cold, droughts and floods, its austerity and indifference. To survive in the desert, one cannot permit oneself distractions, and Ben is the most focused person I have ever met. When he looks at me, I feel that he is looking through me—through my masks, over my walls, and into the depths of my heart. Such insightfulness disarms. His judgments almost always seem right, and even when they don't, they are worthy of careful consideration.

Ben speaks with a deeply grounded knowledge that stems from his people's traditions and land. This is not to say that Ben's beliefs are parochial, narrow, or insular. If anything, they are cosmopolitan, universal, and dynamic. Ben's perspectives, while emerging from and rooted in a particular place, are nonetheless connected to enduring, compelling ethical stances. His life suggests a "rooted cosmopolitanism."[21] The moral authority of his beliefs transcends place even as the beliefs themselves are given shape by place.

Ben's certainty is unusual in our midst. It stands out and puzzles us. A few years after my trip to the Navajo Nation, Ben spoke to my class at Vassar, and one student commented to me, "It's strange to talk to someone who really *knows* what he's saying." Trying not to take the comment personally, I asked my student for clarification. "It's just odd to bump into someone who really believes he knows how things fit together—knows that something is right or wrong."

I noticed a similar reaction in my students when I took them to visit a Bruderhof community in Rifton, New York, in the Catskill Mountains thirty minutes north of Vassar. The

Bruderhof is a Christian commune; its members work, eat, play, sing, and learn in community. This group is difficult for Vassar students to place on their maps of political correctness. On the one hand, the Bruderhof is socially progressive: its members have staunchly opposed the death penalty, the embargo against Cuba, the wars in Iraq and Afghanistan, the military-industrial complex, and all manner of racism and economic injustice. They also raise their own organic food and provide for people with disabilities. All this, Vassar students understand and applaud. Yet on the other hand, the Bruderhof members show little interest in asserting individuality, the women all wear headscarves, and moreover, they call themselves followers of Jesus (having become uneasy with the word "Christian," due to events and politics often associated with Christianity). Most Vassar students are deeply suspicious of religion unless it is private spirituality and all but imperceptible to the outside world. At the Bruderhof, in contrast, there is little that is private.

The Bruderhof posed something of a conundrum for my students. What they found most baffling was the members' self-possession in belief and practice. The Bruderhof members know what they believe, why they believe it, and how they have come to believe it. Yet there is no hint of arrogance or infallibility. My students remarked that they seemed both self-assured and humble. During a meal many years ago at the Bruderhof, I remember an older member told me that the entire community had studied Newt Gingrich's *Contract with America* for several weeks. They had read the entire book communally during their Sunday mornings together, figuring that since the book was written by a congressman on a significant topic, it was appropriate that they read it. I'll never forget her account of the community's assessment of the book and the gentleness with which she spoke it. "You know, Mark, we tried very hard. But we could not find anything of value in that book by the congressman."

Confidence and humility—it's an attractive combination, but

it can unsettle those of us accustomed to a manner of speech and behavior constantly attenuated by qualification, hesitation, evasion, and the ever-present disclaimer, "This is only my opinion."

My students are both attracted to and wary of people who are so secure in their beliefs that they don't show a hint of moral paralysis. Most of us are not rooted in a specific place and set of traditions, and this may be why we do not tend to *know* things in the same way, with the same certitude, as do those who live in tightly knit educative communities. Our way has its advantages. We tend to be broad-minded, morally flexible, and suspicious of dogma. But we pay a price. We live with much doubt and irresoluteness in our lives, especially about who we are—about our identity, our moral orientation, and our trajectory in a socially complex world.

At Stanford I took up the practice of running. I would speed around Palo Alto and Menlo Park, pushing myself harder and harder, telling myself, "This is the pace you need to sustain to get a tenure-track job." I applied this stride to my work, indefatigably reading, writing, and teaching as if I were training for an Olympic event. My life was organized to maximize my study time. When I rested, it was in service of my work.

Sleep is a tortuous challenge for single-minded academicians. We place a high premium on it, because our best work, pace Nietzsche, usually follows a good night's sleep. It's not easy to read Wittgenstein on five hours of sleep, much less to write about his philosophy. And so at bedtime there are a thousand voices in our heads all shouting the same thing: "Sleep! Sleep now to wake up early and alert." It's amazing how some of life's great pleasures—recreation, food, even sex—can become calculated means to a narrow, utilitarian end. In my case, I played, ate, and made love to maintain health for the sake of sustained work—reading, writing, and teaching about the art of living!

Deirdre's lifestyle and mine were compatible. While I was immersed in my academic work, she was occupied with her own, working on an advanced degree in biology at San Francisco State University. And if I put in more hours at work, as I usually did, she relished the time to herself—time for novels, running, hiking, daydreaming. She thrived on the silence in our apartment and when we were in each other's presence, quietly turning the page or stroking the keyboard, we were each comforted by the other's nearness and utter familiarity.

And I did continue to love genuinely the life of learning and teaching. I still read with a passion for the words on the page, for the thrill of the unfolding argument. Yet these *intrinsically* worthy endeavors—love of learning, love of others, love of life—were constantly threatened by what felt like a looming, *extrinsically* imposed objective—a tenure-track position that would allow me to spend the rest of my life immersed in what I loved.

At Stanford, the army of temporary faculty—adjunct instructors, visiting lecturers, and acting professors—would frequently attempt to ingratiate themselves to the institution, offering up their lives in hopes of a stable position. I was no exception, except that I did not offer my life so much to Stanford as to the broader institution of academia: I would go from Stanford to whatever tenure-track was offered me. Don't get me wrong—I would have loved to stay. My parents were there. And the Bay Area has deep hooks in me. Wherever I go, I feel the pull of its light and air, its coastal mountains and cold oceans, redwood forests and sage scrub, grassy valleys and green bay. Even the flashing traffic lights on El Camino work like a homing device, calling me back. I have tried to resist the pull. But the Bay Area will always be beckoning.

Still, as a *visiting* professor at Stanford I believed that my true home lay not in a particular place but in an academic life. If Stanford were to become that true home, I would need to leave to be invited back. During my second year at Stanford an invitation arrived—a tenure-track offer from Vassar College.

On a cold December day, I had my on-campus interview at Vassar with Jack Glasse, the Chair of the department of religion. After a transcontinental flight to JFK, a train ride to Poughkeepsie, a two-hour interview at Vassar, and a late-night walk with Jack around the campus—a two-hundred acre arboretum with perfectly positioned Georgian and Gothic buildings—I bid Jack goodnight and watched him walk up a gently sloped, tree-lined path to his home on college grounds. The air was cold, the pines fragrant, the lamps along the path glinting faintly off the snow. As I watched Jack Glasse ascend quietly to his home on that grand Vassar campus, I saw my dream life for the first time—clear, material, personified, and very close. "A man's dreams are virtually never realized," Wittgenstein once remarked.[22] He was wrong. For fourteen years, I traveled on Jack's path. At Vassar, I received tenure, was promoted to full professor, and served as Chair of the department. I lived what I had dreamt.

Three years after the southwest trip, I met Ben Barney at the Poughkeepsie train station. Instead of driving him directly to the campus center where he would speak and eventually sleep, I drove to my house. I wanted him to see where I lived, to visit my gardens, chickens, turkeys, and bees. I wanted him to walk the path through the woods to the campus with me. Looking back, I know what I was trying to do. I wanted to situate my life for Ben, to show him a snapshot of my soul, to say, "Look, here I am: a person who enjoys a simple lifestyle, who lives close to the earth, walks to work, knows the names of the local trees and shrubs. Look, I am grounded and at home here in Poughkeepsie, New York." (And oh, how hard I would work to be at home in Poughkeepsie, New York!)

On the walk through the woods to campus, Ben asked trenchant questions about who I am, who my people are, what I believe in. I provided answers, confident in them at first. But Ben then asked a series of follow-up questions, deeper queries about elemental things. I floundered. I stammered. With Ben, evasion is not an option. I had to admit that I still didn't know enough about who I was or why I did what I did. I realized that I didn't know enough about my practices, beliefs, traditions—about my people. I needed to work on these things before they worked on me. I needed to prepare for the next time I was to meet Ben. This book, I suppose, is part of that preparation.

After visiting my class, Ben gave a public lecture to a large audience at Vassar. In response to a student's question, Ben told the story of a young man who had contacted him from Pennsylvania and asked to study with Ben in the Navajo Nation. The young man said he needed to get his life together and was sure that Ben and his fellow Navajos could provide the answers he needed. Ben asked him about his family and relatives in Pennsylvania. He asked about his home, his skills, his traditions. He wanted to help the caller to understand that what he needed was probably not far away or foreign in nature, but familiar and close to home. Eventually, the young man's vague responses prompted Ben to ask, "What's going on in Pennsylvania? What's happened to Pennsylvania?"

What's happened to Pennsylvania? What's happened to the U.S.? What's happened to plurality of local cultures and practices? What provides for a sense of history, meaning, and future? It's easy to be cynical, I know. It's easy to look sentimentally on other cultures and judge our own harshly. There are plenty of problems in Ben's Navajo culture and plenty of strengths in my own. Yet there are things his culture does well that my culture needs help with. My-kind-and-I have lost many of the public and private practices that emerge from a knowledge of place, community, traditions, and self.

Of course, a deep sense of place is not the answer to every question or problem. There are times when maturation requires that we leave our place in order to return to it with new understanding and vision. This can happen, and this did happen to Ben.

During his visit to my class, Ben told my students a story about a man waiting for a train. Looking over his heavy load of assorted baggage, he decided to discard one bag, and then another, and so on. By the time he boarded the train, he had in his possession only a small carry-on. The man in the story was Ben, and that train took him from the Navajo Nation to an airport, where he boarded a flight for Germany and a year of professional dance.

As Ben described the process of unburdening his past to travel into his future, my students and I breathed in his words—his message was simple, direct, honest, and powerful. In Arizona, Ben had left behind his language, family, traditions, and nation. He had discarded his baggage—those sources of comfort, security, and identity we so often cling to.

So much for my Navajo example of a man firmly embedded in tradition and place. Ben's flight to Germany is rather inconvenient for the sake of that narrative. But then, perhaps his journey from home has something to do with the depth of his local knowledge. To cross to safety we sometimes need to hazard risks and give up what is safest and dearest. Our relinquishment may be only temporary. We may eventually receive everything back. But we can never know such things in advance. Some of us may need to set our house on fire just to get home.

Ben's presence had power over my students and me. His words woke us up. That evening, I received a knock on my office door from Lauren, a first semester freshman. Given that it was late and I had never talked to her outside of class, I was surprised and even a little irritated to see her. I had work to do, for Ben's presence had consumed my entire day (and then some). Yet how could I fail to welcome the earnest student who said by way of greeting, "Mr. Cladis, I need your advice on something." I looked up from my work, our eyes met, and I said, "Let me guess. You want to drop out of Vassar and live in Nepal." "Yes," she replied—and without a hint of astonishment, as if people often knew what she was going to say before she said it.

I recollect well the impression Lauren made on me. She was hungry not for sheer excitement and adventure—she understood how the lure of exotic travel can leave us feeling as hollow as ever. No, Lauren was eager to encounter the basics in life, the fundamentals. And like Ben, she felt the need to leave much behind in order to look on her own life with greater perspective.

Looking back, I'm surprised I didn't try to dissuade her. Surely her parents might have wanted that. She was only eighteen years old and had been at Vassar less than two months. It might have appeared that she was hastily running from, not thoughtfully moving toward, something else. Yet I supported her decision. Her speech was thoughtful. Her words suggested considerable maturity and self-knowledge. She was not naïve about the difficulties she would encounter abroad. My main concern, I remember, was not about her leaving but about her returning.

As a teacher, I've been forced to accept that education—including classroom learning—often entails disruption. Learning and love entail the risk of unsettlement. Emerson must have had something like this in mind when he wrote, "People wish to be settled; only as far as they are unsettled is there any hope for them."[23] If we are genuinely searching, we can't keep holding out for comfort.

I brought to Vassar the carefully constructed life I had built at Stanford—living cautiously and living for my work. At Stanford, of course, there had been the terrifying possibility of not securing a tenure-track position anywhere. But I could manage and defeat the risk, I thought, by hard work. My running stride would outstrip any obstacles and carry me over the finish line. It was my pace, I believed, that had earned me the Vassar tenure-track position, and it would be my pace that would eventually win me tenure itself, professional security—a riskless life.

Looking back, while I see a correlation between my work (publications) and my academic success (tenure at an elite liberal arts college), I now see something else, too. I see others like me, just as smart or smarter, working as hard or harder, whose work and talent does not grant them the same success in academia. I see all of us running in place, pushing up against a gate, and then—all at once, magically, mysteriously—the gate opens enough for a single one of us to pass through. Those let into the hallowed grounds never hear the gate crashing behind them, and their memories of the gate vanish. They remember only their hard work, high marks on exams, and teachers' praise. As memory of the gate fades, so does the gratitude for its brief aperture and the dread of its mysterious operations.

By the time I came to Vassar, I had grown ponderous. Buoyancy, vitality, risk-taking—I had traded those for a plodding routine and the compulsion to publish. But change came, luckily, prior to tenure, before I was given that lifetime key to the university's gates—after which perhaps I would have never looked back. During those first years at Vassar, I was given a remarkable opportunity: a chance to wake up, to remember things I once knew, and to address my spiritual poverty before it was too late.

At the end of the fall semester, Lauren left for the northeast region of Nepal. For six months she lived with a family in the small village of Juving, where she taught English, built compost toilets, and led evening courses for mothers. Lauren traveled light, having left behind most of her burdens. When she returned to Vassar, she was even lighter—more self-possessed, confident, grounded, and happier. In Nepal, Lauren gained a deepened sense of purpose, a clearer sense of what is significant in her life and what is not. I saw in her something of what

I saw in Ben Barney: the ease of one who carries within only what is needful.

At the time, I was still carrying much, a camel saddled for a journey through the desert. I had not gained the ability to distinguish, effortlessly, things that mattered from things that didn't. I was still unsure what to let go of.

Robert Frost unapologetically held on to some personal possessions, and why not?

> I could give all to Time except—except
> What I myself have held. But why declare
> The things forbidden that while the Customs slept
> I have crossed to Safety with? For I am There
> And what I would not part with I have kept.[24]

Not everything should or can be discarded. Even the monk who takes a vow of poverty and casts off all possessions still carries with him some vestiges of his past—memories that none should consider contraband. There are some experiences we should not be willing to let go of. We declare, "These are mine!" and no other argument for possession is required. Thus Frost pronounces the perfect tautology: "What I would not part with I have kept." It is a threadbare life that has shed its memories, whether they be strands of joy or pain.

In *safety*, memories serve to remind us of who we were and what we wish to become. In *safety*, we can handle those memories that at other times we would prefer to run from or ignore. In *safety*, reflection on our past is suffused with a quiet meaning that, even if painful, is life-affirming. In *safety*, personal memory is to an individual what tradition is to a people: a safe repository we dip into on a variety of occasions for hope or comfort, for guidance or understanding, or just for pleasure. In *safety*, we do not hide from life, from tragedy or loss; we face it while holding on to what we have kept—and what has kept us.

❧

When we think of transformation, we usually think of abrupt change. The fairy godmother appears. The lottery is won. The plane crash is survived. My transformation, in contrast, was incremental, piecemeal, and plural in its sources. There were the Vassar students. There was a family. There were the chickens and bees. There was Paul. And so at Vassar, before tenure and before the end of my marriage, I was offered diverse avenues of change.

The Vassar students showed none of the deference of the Greensboro students. At Greensboro, I was *Dr. Cladis*; at Vassar I was *Mr. Cladis* and sometimes *Mark*. Vassar students are bright, individualistic, and creative. They are also a little kooky, and in time they shaped me in their own image. I brought to Vassar such courses as Religion and Critical Inquiry and The History of Christian Thought. After a few years there, I was teaching Religion Gone Wild: Spirituality and the Environment and Love: the Concept and Practice. With a new line-up of courses, I found that I could now offer the students something that wasn't listed on the syllabus. I could offer myself—and invite them to do the same. I still had many shortcomings as a teacher. But I was making a start.

Baggage makes its claims on both students and teachers. It is easy to bring to class woundable egos, insecurities, the rigid directives of former teachers, and the towering expectations of parents. But there are some things we *should* bring with us. In the classroom, I invoke my favorite teachers. They are with me as I teach, alongside my friends and family members, and the philosophers, authors, and poets who have inspired me. Then there are my stories and an assortment of victories and disappointments—these, too, I bring to the classroom. Bowen Brown, my best friend in junior high school, helps me illustrate Aristotle's theory of friendship. My grandmother, Mary Cladis, and her bar, *Mary's Place*, help me depict the struggles and triumphs of women immigrants. Present too is the philosopher Wittgenstein and his claim that we never exist radically alone; the novelist Zora Neale Hurston and her portrayal of grace in the face of hardship; the poet Mary Oliver and her illumination of the necessity and beauty of death—these thinkers are with me all the time. And so is Paul Kane. I often find myself wondering, both in and out of the classroom, what would Paul do in this situation.

We seldom do anything from scratch. Whether we are cooking, teaching, or loving, there is always some precedent, history, or influence. In the past lie our dearest resources and our greatest burdens. My question of what to keep and what to leave behind is rarely a choice requiring a decision and subsequent action. It is more a condition that must be addressed and negotiated daily. It requires practice, skillfulness, and consciousness. It requires receptivity to our future and respect for our past. Perhaps near the end of my life, I will know what to let go of and how.

On the second morning of our visit to the Navajo Nation, Ben declared to Paul and me that he wants to die with no habits. He wants to cull his habits, day by day, until none remain. I was making pancakes at the time, trying hard to remember the *Joy of Cooking* recipe (Is it one and one half or one and three quarters teaspoons baking powder?). At that moment, I was wishing I had practiced more the habit of making pancakes. "That would be a hard way to live," I told him, "having to approach each situation completely anew. A human without habits is like an organism without reflexes. One would need to remember at each moment how to breathe, swallow, blink, and so on. One would be incapable of living."

Habit and religion, or at least habit and spirituality, are often seen as opposites. In this view, habits involve mindless routine whereas spirituality necessitates mindful awareness. Yet I wonder. Many religious traditions have cultivated spiritual practices, which, like habits, are often routines that, once acquired, demand little thought. Indeed, often the purpose of a religious practice is to occupy the mind with an ingrained series of thoughts so that we might contemplatively attend to that inward, quiet world beyond, or at least distinct from, discursive thinking. But more likely, the practice itself is its own reward.

There are days when, walking home from work, disquietude follows me from the office, shadowing my every move. Was I too abrupt with that colleague? Did I truly grasp that student's question? Should I revise the rejected article or submit it elsewhere? On these days when I can't seem to let go of my burdens, I am especially grateful for a practice, a *form*, that I can enter. This routine of mine (something of a prescribed, meditative walking practice) liberates me from the need to be spiritually inspired in the moment. I am not inspired; I am cranky and tired and fed-up. But I know the routine. And so, feeling dull, I enter it and eventually it enters me, and the world, inside and out, changes a bit.

I could appreciate Ben's comment if he meant that he wanted to rid himself of *bad* habits. But he had in mind something deeper, more fundamental, more radical. He wants to root out all mechanical actions and gestures, all assumptions and prejudices. His goal is to become an individual who at each moment is wholly intentional, fully aware of his every word, every action—maybe even every breath.

I had protested that to live without habits is to have to approach every situation anew. Yet that must be exactly what Ben desires: to meet every circumstance as if for the first time, responding appropriately and not by rote; to discard "the veil of familiarity" and experience newness in every moment. He desires to become the open-minded child who expects the unexpected, while remaining the wise adult who knows how to behave when faced with surprise.

Once again, Ben Barney the Navajo fails to live up to my stereotype of the Native American set firmly in his people's traditions, customs, and habits. He identifies with Navajo ways and exhibits Navajo habits—his gestures, his walk, his patience, for instance—but his identification with Navajo ways is intentional and his habits are mostly benign patterns deriving more from muscle memory than inattention. Ben's goal, in addition to becoming consummately attentive and intentional, relates to the redefinition of his social identity: to become so thoroughly and self-consciously Navajo that he could, when appropriate, knowingly suspend any of his cultural traditions.

He is not attempting to shed his Navajo ways. On the contrary, he is traveling to the depths of Navajo traditions and in those extremities finding and enjoying others who have traveled to the depths of their own traditions. In those deep regions, these journeyers might discover a common humanity as cultural prejudice and even habits seem to soften, melt, and perhaps vanish. I have yet to join them there. I can barely imagine the journey.

I received a letter from Ben about a year after his visit to Vassar. It felt well-timed.

> Mark,
>
> What in the world are you doing? What have you been through? What has changed and what has stayed the same? Even when everything is moving on and the days are always bringing new things, a person can stay the same. I see that all the time.
>
> In September I had the peyote ceremony and it brought me a new inner sense that surprised me. There is again the sense of what I come from and where I am rooted: that is here. My house represents a way of being that is me and that is not going anywhere. The belief and faith is inside me and is no longer following anything or anyone; but it only is within me. It just sits there if I do nothing with it and it waits till it decays into nothingness. It is very much like life; if nothing is done with it, it dies and withers. The

> house I have is like that faith and belief; the house begins to fall apart if I am doing little to nothing with it. Soon, there is only history and dry air. That seems to be the way things are whether it be inside or outside the self.

When we seek a course, whether for a classroom or a life, we ask of it two things: that it lead to the *steadiness* of a developed self and the *fluidity* of an expanding self.

This twofold movement—down into age-old bedrock and up into open sky—is what Ben has written of. In our tutorials—that is, his visits to Poughkeepsie and mine to Lukachukai—I am reminded of the need to be both grounded and unleashed. Before some truth can set us free, we must plant our feet in truthfulness, goodness, and honesty. But once secure, we must let ourselves grow, ascend, and develop, and the new vistas we encounter will place even our groundwork in new perspective.

In Ben's letter and life, there is an inventive and intricate dance embracing stillness and motion, standing like a mountain and soaring like a hawk. This dance, as I now understand it, is part of the search for a course. Ben's letter suggests that what we acquire in the way of conviction and understanding, "belief and faith," requires renovation and maintenance. It also requires rest and nourishment to grow. And finally, if the grandeur of the interior space is to prevail, it must be shared.

This lesson in hospitality might seem redundant to an educator. After all, aren't teachers forever imparting? Yet as educators we are trained to impart only a highly limited, specialized portion of what we have come to know and understand. There are good reasons for respecting these boundaries. Pedagogical discretion accepts that any curriculum is necessarily limited. Education can become coercion when teachers fail to recognize limits, misuse their authority, and present their personal doctrines as "The Way." Still, there are occasions when we should be willing to offer students something beyond our narrow, specialized training—not necessarily more of our personal lives (though that may be appropriate at times), but certainly more of our wide-ranging reflections and narratives about what we have come to find significant, troubling, horrific, or beautiful in our social, moral, and physical worlds.

Pedagogical discretion. What to tell? What to hold back? In my course, Love: the Concept and Practice, there is a two-week section on marriage. We discuss the relationship between marriage, friendship, and *eros*. We read Aristotle, Dante, de Rougemont, and Wallace Stegner. We watch *The Return of Martin Guerre* and *The Crying Game*. We talk about marriage and the futility of attempting to dodge, rather than navigate, marital change. Change tiptoed into my marriage and then toppled it with a body blow.

Do I tell my story to my students? Should I tell them *everything* I know about marriage? Do I pull from my backpack the crumpled piece of paper that for years I carried with me as a reminder, a warning:

> Stopple the orifices of your heart,
> Close your doors;
>   your whole life you will not suffer.
> Open the gate of your heart…
>   your whole life you will be beyond salvation.[25]

Do I tell my students why I wrote it down and held it close? Do I tell them that when one begins to suffer, the way out of sorrow is often detachment from those relationships that inevitably lead to suffering? Do I talk of the years before the catastrophe, of Deirdre's growing silence, of my prayers for words—some syllables of life—and of my sadness as I would count inwardly each word she offered me? Do I talk of that vague sense that a secret was building a soundproof partition between us? And do I speak of the fear of asking my wife, "Do you love me?" and of her tears and speechless sorrow? What to tell?

The time Paul and I spent with Ben Barney was lively, rich, and productive. For our course at Vassar, we learned about the Anasazi (ancestral Pueblo peoples) who lived a thousand years ago in the Canyon De Chelly. We visited the Navajo farms that still dot the floor of the canyon, and we witnessed firsthand how the marvel of that place is made still more "intense," as Ansel Adams noted, by the presence of the Navajo. Yes, we came to appreciate Adams's claim that the Navajo of the Canyon de Chelly "demonstrate that man can live with nature and sometimes enhance it."[26] Ben told stories illustrating the pragmatic relation between the Navajo and their land. This Navajo pragmatism, which refuses to reduce the land to a distant, sublime landscape estranged from the practical affairs of human community, shows profound aesthetic and spiritual dimensions. Together we saw the antecedents of Navajo place names that have endured for centuries, and we observed the pattern of family homes inscribing the land with lines of complex Navajo kinship. During the days, we hiked in the desert, down deep canyons and up steep cliff trails. In the evenings, we cooked delicious meals, talked about serious matters, and sometimes laughed until we wept.

And then there were the stars. On our last night together we pulled out the star charts, ventured into the dark desert, and searched the dazzling sky. At first we had a hard time matching the charts with the time, season, and celestial sector of our sky. Eventually the stars lined up and we began to name them—first with their Greek and Roman names, later with their Navajo names. Was this our way of honoring the heavens, or taming them?

We often want to touch beautiful things—a soft cat, a sweet child, a gentle lover. We want to draw near to beautiful things, because our lives long for beauty. When I was a child, I used to look out of my tiny bedroom window for hours. Out that window was the richest ensemble of trees and flowers, all stunningly colored in every season. Yet somehow the sight was so beautiful it *hurt.* Yes, beauty can cause pain. It can wound. Perhaps because we can't hold those grand, faraway objects of beauty—mountains or stars—we are wounded by ineffability and want. Perhaps all objects of beauty participate in that quality of not-being-held. And if we can't hold what is beautiful, we at least try to name it. The habit of naming runs deep.

I suppose during that last night together, we were, in our own way, trying to hold some stars. In the end, however, there was nothing to do but put down the charts and gaze in silence.

In spite of my weekly lunch meetings with Paul and a more vital approach to teaching, my life felt increasingly barren. What do we do when we are desperate for *life*—for the messiness of it all, the laugher and yelps, the noise and chaos, the thousand-and-one tangible expressions of love and connection? Do we have an affair? Not if we're faithful. Do we go to marriage counseling? Not if our spouse refuses. Do we fight? Only in silence. From where, then, does the life flow? In time, life reached me in the form of a family with seven home-schooled children, wise parents, and a plenitude of love and bustle.

Here's how it happened. Vassar put up for sale one of its college homes, on the same hill that I had seen Jack Glasse climb years before. I loved the location, the first- and second-generation woods with dry stack stone walls here and there, reminders of former farm fields and past lives. But Deirdre and I worried about the immediate neighbors to the north. They had kids and lots of them. Also, they never seemed to be in school, and would incessantly run around in the yard, making a racket. I knew all this because for two months prior to buying the vacated home, I had set up a lawn chair on the back deck and read and wrote for hours. Buying a house is a big deal, so I was trying out what I took to be its most important feature: the prospect for peace and quiet, its conduciveness to reading and writing. The scenery was inspiring, but the noise from "that Walker family" never stopped. Squeals of delight, children's audible plans of intrigue, the construction of forts in the woods, and the live music—guitars and fiddles, harmonicas and accordions, tambourines and recorders, even a bagpipe!

I remember talking to my sister-in-law about it. "I love everything about the house but that family next door is going to drive me to distraction." "Mark, my guess is you'll all become best friends." I resented her glad tidings; what did she know of peace and quiet with her three children? Still, in the end, Deirdre and I bought the house.

One day shortly after we moved in, as I was walking to work, I passed Kathy Walker—mother, farmer, wise matriarch—outside her home with a large cast-iron skillet of cornbread. With a few children at her side, she offered me a golden chunk with homemade butter. How could I resist? In time, I discovered what was truly irresistible: the Walker children—all seven of them. I knew it the first time little Forest Walker slipped his hand in my hand as if it belonged there. I knew it when we swam together in the Hudson, hiked in Minnewaska, picnicked at North Lake, contra-danced in the Arlington Reformed Church, and flew a remote-controlled airplane, the same oft-mended aircraft that survived an entire winter in a Chestnut tree only to be retrieved and flown again in spring. Within a year, I had become an honorary member of their clan. They loved me, and I was changed by their love.

My heart broke at the end of our year together. The Walkers decided to leave Poughkeepsie and start a farm near Seattle, where they had family. Jeff Walker, a colleague in the geology department, took a "leave of absence" from Vassar; they sold their home; each child packed a two-by-two box of personal items; they loaded a trailer; and on a mid-July morning at 4:00 a.m., they headed West.

I had left a note for them on the trailer hitch—it couldn't be missed. When I awoke, I went to the spot where the trailer had been parked. There on the ground, secured by a rock, was a handmade card in the penmanship of the children. They had known, somehow, that I would go back to that place.

Days Seven and Eight

Drive back to Farmington; visits to Shiprock with William and Vida Clift

We had packed our rental car and said our goodbyes when Ben suddenly asked if we would be willing to take something with us. What souvenir would this wise man have us take away to remember him by? Lorain had given us sage and a shell to burn it in. What would Ben present? He returned from his house with two large bags of garbage. He wondered if we would be willing to toss them in a dumpster on our way to Farmington, New Mexico, our next destination.

This was now our second visit to Farmington. It would serve as our home base for excursions to Shiprock with Bill Clift and his wife, Vida. At breakfast the next morning at the Riverwalk Patio & Grill, I met Vida for the first time. I was not surprised to discover that she was smart, inquisitive, and possessed of a quiet intensity similar to Bill's. Remarkable people, I have found, often couple up. Vida is simply beautiful, in mind and body. Her face radiates kindness, perspicacity, and something I'm tempted to call "awakeness." That's not a very pretty noun, I know, but it conveys best what I saw then and see now. It's also part of what is indescribable about Paul's face and Bill's. When we encounter someone who looks fully awake, it's noticeable—perhaps because most of us navigate our worlds half-asleep, accustomed to the faces of fellow sleepwalkers. Awakeness is not that quality following a good night's sleep or a cup of coffee or the receipt of good news. It's the subtle, undeniable, noncontingent alertness I see in all three faces.

After our early breakfast in the dark and the forty-five-minute drive to Shiprock in Bill and Vida's Land Rover, the sun had yet to rise. In the crisp, predawn air, Bill prepared to photograph Shiprock's east face. I've been in the presence of professional photographers who quickly shoot a roll of film, their cameras sounding like popping corn. But Bill's camera is mostly silent. He uses little film, takes few shots, and spends much time studying the view. So on that morning, desiring to capture Shiprock before sunrise, Bill patiently surveyed the land, set up his box camera, loaded the five-by-seven film, and took a single photograph in the fifteen minutes before the sun emerged from the horizon.

I took a photo, too. In it, Shiprock is dark and silver, quiet and serene, and somewhat forbidding. If it wasn't for a slight sheen of pink in the background, its appearance would be altogether inhospitable. It seems to say, "You may look, but don't touch."

Shortly after sunrise we returned to the Land Rover—a stalwart photographic workshop on wheels whose strength and simplicity reminded me of Bill and Vida themselves. We drove around to Shiprock's north side, where we began our ascent on foot, carrying with us the large box camera, tripod, and two cases of photographic supplies. After climbing for a couple of hours, I took a picture of the group. In it Vida, Bill, and Paul stand on the rocky slope with equipment in hand, while far beneath them a dark speck—the Land Rover—floats on an ocean of sand. It's impossible not to think of the desert surrounding Shiprock as aquatic. In every direction it reaches out to meet the horizon and its dips and swells are like beige, rolling waves.

The name Shiprock is not incidental to this oceanic landscape. Supposedly, early white settlers in the 1870s saw a resemblance between the rock and a windjammer under full sail. I see it myself. But it is the high, oceanic sands that make the "ship" float. Take them away and it becomes something else.

It *is* something else to the Navajo. To their eyes it was never a ship in an ocean. Why would the desert look like an ocean to a people with little exposure to oceans and much exposure to deserts? To the Navajo the desert looked like a desert—not the empty, boundless wasteland of the Euro-American imagination, but an abode replete with various animal, plant, and human communities. And the rock—that magnificent igneous intrusion—looked to them like *Tsé Bit' a' i'*, a Winged Rock.

Tsé Bit' a' i' is a place that speaks of deliverance and loss, of promising beginnings and painful endings. It spoke *of* my life at the time. And eventually, it spoke *to* it.

It was Kathy Walker who said, "Mark's not a friend; he's family." The large family and I had been crammed in their van—a van that smelled of children, chickens, and sheep—heading up Route Nine for a day hike. I remember rebuffing Kathy: "No," I said, "I'm a family friend." Why reject Kathy's kind and harmless familial designation? Without knowing it, Kathy had named my worry that the Walkers were becoming a surrogate family to me. Deirdre would occasionally join us on the outings, but it was always with more effort than joy. What had become my great delight—spending time with this troop of vibrant children and their parents—was increasingly a chore for her. I began to see that my relationship with the Walkers was risky—that it gave me an excuse to evade the difficulties of my own family by becoming part of theirs. Jeff and Kathy had become some of my closest friends, and I loved the children—Peter, Laurel, Mary-Claire, Patrick, Forest, Rachel, and Hannah—as if they were my own. For my own sake, then, I corrected Kathy: "I'm a family friend."

Before I met the Walkers, children were a foreign species—and not an especially attractive one. Why would I want to enter the noisy, chaotic world of children? I felt that my world and the world of parents were radically incommensurate. Two worlds unable to be bridged.

The Walker children were a bridge. They gave me the chance

to enter the world of children, to hold their hands, hear their stories, wipe their tears. The Walkers showed me what I could hope for. And that is one of the most powerful gifts one can give.

❧

Tsé Bit' a' i' is a sacred place that can fascinate—simultaneously entice and frighten—with its grave appearance and history in Navajo belief. Many legends refer to *Tsé Bit' a' i'*, but the most famous is set in a time when the Navajo, the Diné, were persecuted by their enemies. The *Hataałii* (medicine men) prayed for help, and the Holy Ones heard their plea. The earth heaved and released a great bird that carried the Diné eastward on its back. Having delivered the Diné to safety, the great bird turned into stone, where it remains today.

The Diné's winged deliverer soon became their home. They dwelled on the rock, coming down to fetch water and tend crops. One day while the men were working the fields below, a terrible storm descended and lightning struck Winged Rock, leaving sheer cliff where the trail had been. The men below could not ascend, and the women, children, and old men above could not come down. The tribe was split, fatally. Everyone on the rock slowly starved to death, and there their corpses remain.

From bird to stone, from home to graveyard, Winged Rock underwent its own inexorable metamorphosis. The story goes with the place, and the place with the story. Winged Rock keeps its distance, and keeps much else as well. It should be approached with respect and caution.

During our several visits to Shiprock, I often wondered where the Navajo were. Now I understand why they were absent. To them, *Tsé Bit' a' i'* is as dangerous as it is sacred. And climbing *Tsé Bit' a' i'* could only be foolish and disrespectful. The Navajo protested vehemently against climbers from the Sierra Club who scaled Shiprock's steep face to its peak in October of 1939. One must not disturb the *chʼį́įdii* (ghosts) of the stranded. Since then it has become illegal to climb.

All this I learned after my visits. Yet from the way my companions comported themselves, I understood that we walked on hallowed ground. We behaved as if we were visiting a church or mosque in a foreign land. In our own places of worship, we might feel free to act somewhat casually. But as guests in a sacred place, we are especially attentive and self-conscious, walking slowly, speaking softly, listening carefully, and gazing intently. If we laughed on Shiprock, we did so quietly. But I don't remember any laughter.

I do remember much silence. We were quiet, watchful visitors on a brief passage through a holy site. We were aware, always, of the centuries of dishonor and devastation white people had wrought on Native Americans. And yet there we were, practically trespassers—a poet, a philosopher, a photographer, a priestess.

Why were we there? Many reasons. Vida loves this Southwest landscape and would never miss an opportunity to spend time in it—not just gazing at it from a car but moving bodily in and through it. Paul and Bill, who share Vida's love of the Southwest, were there for professional reasons. They had been collaborating on a book about Shiprock and Mont St. Michel, exploring through verse and photography the relationship of these two majestic, rocky sites. This excursion would be their last joint visit to Shiprock before the book's completion. Bill had some final photographs to shoot, and Paul had a few poems yet to write.

And then there was the matter of that team-taught course. Although Paul and I did not expect Shiprock to play a significant role in the syllabus, it made sense that, given the title—Contemplation in the American Landscape—we ought to devote some time to fieldwork: contemplating in an American landscape.

There's actually a lot of pressure on a professor who dares to offer a course with such a title. It's not as easy as it sounds. When and where and how does the contemplating begin? Must it happen in solitude? Do I sit or stand? Face the east or the west? If my eyes are open, are they focused or roaming or relaxed to the point of blurriness? If my eyes are closed, is my attention on the wind on my skin or the rustle in my ears? And what is the goal? Deep insight, strong feeling, renewed strength, a quiet mind? Or perhaps the idea of a goal is misguided?

How does a contemplative novice begin his journey toward serenity? How does a man in crisis start to search for inner peace? Can one ever become a specialist in the experience of the sublime? A contemplation consultant? A licensed meditator? People do of course train and practice contemplative exercises for years and years. The Thomas Mertons and Thich Nhat Hahns have grasped something truthful and profoundly significant about the nature of life that most of us have yet to recognize. They do speak with much skill and objectivity about contemplative life. I know "objectivity" isn't a term usually associated with contemplation, but when I read the works of these expert teachers, I have the unmistakable impression that they are reporting factually on what is indeed the case. They've got it right.

Regarding my own contemplative progress, I did advance. It's not surprising. There is nothing mysterious about such improvement. Proficiency in contemplation is like proficiency in anything: it takes practice and a good teacher. We must be taught the basics—techniques in breathing, principles of posture, lessons in concentration and attitude. At first it is difficult and we are unsure. But persist, and we improve. It's that simple. This learning to learn was part of my search for a course.

About two months before my marital crisis, I wrote a short entry in my journal: "Mayday. *M'aidez*. Help me."

In the film *The Perfect Storm*, when the ship loses its radio antenna in the escalating storm, we hear the captain of its sister ship shout into her radio, "Mayday, Mayday, Mayday!" The danger is as clear as the cry for help. But what do we exclaim when confronted with a vague sense that we are about to freefall—or that we are already falling, but in slow motion? What do we utter in the face of indistinct danger? Looking back, I see there was a grave and imminent threat to my marriage and my life, but when I wrote "Mayday," it was only a confused prayer, an entreaty to survive what I did not yet understand.

Part II

In Search of a Life

With effort, then, anyone can make contemplative progress. Of course, not all of us can call ourselves *Thich*, and not all of us want to. Although natural talent can seldom replace practice, practice takes some further than others. To achieve greatness in any pursuit, grace (natural gifts) and will (commitment) must combine. Few have the patience for greatness. If we are honest with ourselves, we are not interested in the privations and effort that greatness requires. And why should we be? Can't we enjoy contemplation without the goal of utter mastery—*especially* without this goal? If I sit in meditation to imagine that I am Thomas Merton or Shunryu Suzuki, I am living too far outside myself.

Our culture fosters a yearning to become someone else, to put faith in rapid self-transformation facilitated by products and possessions. If we become interested in cycling, for example, we are tempted to purchase a top-of-the-line bike and all the related paraphernalia—sleek pants, gel gloves, titanium tire pump—to bring us closer to the image on the website or catalogue cover. The icon, however, still looms ahead of us, on the other side of still more purchases—better handlebars, lighter wheels, a hydration system. Invariably, the icon remains unreachable and the fantasy falls away. We could genuinely commit, work hard, and become exceptional cyclists; yet still we would fail to attain the life of the icon. Our existence as excellent cyclists would still comprise pain, disappointment, and boredom. Some of us might learn to prefer the reality of an authentic cycling practice; more of us would sooner abandon cycling and chase a new fantasy.

Living in a celebrity culture, we are assaulted daily by the digital and glossy images of heroes of the age—film stars, athletes, musicians, and fashion models. Even if by the most superficial of measures, these images show us where we fall short. They invite us to imagine inhabiting the life and body of the featured hero, and usually promote a product designed to assist us in our reinvention. Our chain pharmacies and online drug stores are well-stocked with potions and charms that promise to cure our various shortcomings—hair too straight or too curly, skin too dry or too oily, complexion too pale or too dark. It is fitting that *pharmacies* dispense these products, which have become, in a sense, cultural *drugs*. While prescriptions are not normally required to purchase them, these products are nonetheless highly addictive. Cosmetics, although applied on the surface, radiate in every direction, penetrating deeply and emanating expansively.

That our market economy and celebrity culture buy and sell images is by now a familiar idea and it has made us obsessed with our bodies. Airbrushed or photoshopped images haunt us, even with the screen off. We gaze at ourselves torturously, women especially but increasingly men, too, as all are subject to the Unworkable Directive: *indulge the self and discipline the body.*

I am more worried about the discipline than the indulgence, though the two are closely related. It may seem indulgent to apply expensive body lotions or to make costly visits to the salon. Such acts could be justified as innocent pampering, a form of healthy self-love. But what do we call liposuction, Botox injections, and breast implants? Anabolic steroids and diet pills? Are these acts of self-love or self-hatred? During grueling workouts at the gym, are we loving our bodies, or are we loving the Perfect Body and punishing our own?

We seek not only the Perfect Body. We strive for the Perfect Life. We dream of living somewhere else, being married to someone else, doing something else, being more like our icons. We offer our hearts to the theater screen, Facebook profile, and magazine page, as if our hearts are not at home in the homes we have made. We have become hollow-chested, vacuous.

In addition to the products manufactured to change our appearances, there are those that treat symptoms of hollow-chestedness: yoga videos, Zen pillows, aromatherapy, antidepressants. Unlike the products that displaced our hearts in the first place, these alternatives often encourage us to embrace the self—pretty much just as it is. Such therapies, then, rarely ask us to make fundamental changes in our lives or to challenge the dysfunctional practices that harry us. Rather, these curatives claim to enable us to defeat the storms and strains endemic to our hectic, perfectionistic culture. With fifteen minutes per day of yoga or meditation, we are told, we can find peace, survive chaos, and accomplish even more each day. What a bargain.

And if we seek "deep, meaningful love," online dating services guarantee to put us in "*control* of romance." Just as we can reshape our eyebrows and torsos, so, too, we can reshape our romantic fates. We can *make* love happen, because, as one site claims, "flirting is fun—but email is where real love connections are made." Love, like online shopping, has been made convenient, quick, and easy, especially with such bonus features as speed-dating and drop-down boxes for body type, income, and creed.

We can have it all is the message of many self-help products and services. We can do it all: shop for groceries, fix the plumbing, pay bills, work out, vote, watch movies, moisturize our skin, work sixty hours a week, date; prepare meals, change diapers, carpool kids, attend PTA meetings, plan and survive the family vacation. We can have health, beauty, love, children, community, recreation, career, and inner well-being—if we only add fifteen minutes of yoga to our crammed daily schedules.

Pursuing these valid objectives is not the problem. Seeking services to help us forge a full and meaningful life is not the problem. My qualm is not with yoga, online dating, or antidepressants; rather, I am worried about a culture and economy that sells images of people unmoved by the challenges of living and dying. I worry about a culture that advertises fantasies. I worry about the promotion of unworkable shortcuts—quick love, easy enlightenment, and rapid wealth.

❧

The Walkers were back. After a year of struggling to make it in the Seattle area, the family moved back to the Hudson River Valley and our family romance resumed exactly where it had left off. In Hyde Park, they bought a modest home on eight acres with a barn and chicken coop. Soon, they acquired chickens, turkeys, ducks, rabbits, sheep, goats, a mule, and a horse. Soon, they were plowing the hay fields, planting the vegetable garden, and, in the evenings, enjoying leisurely summer walks in their back woods. In the winter months, they tapped their sugar maple trees, split hardwood for their cook stove, cross-country skied in the snowy woods, skated on the ice pond, and enjoyed an occasional sleigh ride. Yes, the Walkers had returned, and like the hardy maples in their woods, they offered the sap of life.

Was I wrong to crave sanity and wholesomeness? I sought life, yet in my marriage and even much of my professional life, I subsisted largely on stand-ins for, and alleged shortcuts to, life. Was I wrong, then, to hold on to the Walkers for dear—sweet, real—life?

The family, of course, was a living, breathing counterculture. They made their own clothes from the wool they spun from the fleece they carded from the sheep they sheared. They made cheese with milk from the goats they milked every morning and evening. They homeschooled their seven children without the benefit of iPad applications or the screen babysitter. These unconventional ways, however, were not what made the family so radically alternative. Rather, it was those traits so deeply established in the children's dispositions—kindness, thoughtfulness, and gentleness—that characterized the family's departure from the norm. I don't deny the connection between the life-affirming character of the family and their farming life; yet not all farms produce a Walker family, and not all such families require a farm. Essentially, they require good work, buoyant faith, and unshakable love. I joined them in their work, shared their faith, and was blessed by their love.

❧

I worry about the promotion of unworkable shortcuts in our culture. I also worry about being told that there are no limits to what we can accomplish gracefully within a day or a week or a year. We North Americans have a difficult time with the very idea of limits, often seeking to overcome them with harder, defter work, or else denying them altogether. It seldom occurs to us that working and living well might entail the judicious acceptance of limits.

It amazes me that I keep trying to accomplish more than health and sanity allow. Even when I finally admit my own over-extension, I insist that my state of mind, and not the implausibly busy schedule overflowing my Google calendar, is at fault for my loss of equanimity. My great temptation is to believe that I should focus on, and enjoy, one or two tasks at a time, rather than lament the hundreds of tasks I have yet to accomplish each day. This approach borders on wise counsel, because its objective is to avoid the massive millstone of my many duties, to get out from under its heft in order to delight in and attend to what is before me in the present.

And who would doubt the superiority of delight and attentiveness in the moment over the dread of future chores and impatience with the task at hand? But this approach is a decoy, because it draws our attention away from the condition that predicates our worry and fear. It obscures the need for a *structural*—not purely *mental*—change to address a systemic problem. And what is this problem? The habitual attempt to do more than can be done well and with excellence, comeliness, and grace. It's no use trying to cultivate mindfulness if we refuse to reduce the untenable number of demands in our lives. The mind, however trained, is always embedded in a body and a lifestyle. If this body is fatigued and this lifestyle hectic, so is the mind. In today's culture, achieving a measure of simplicity is our challenge. It is also our hope.

The great temptation I have described—to mitigate the

ache of overextension with mental effort—is held by those who William James called the "healthy-minded." For them, the world outside the self is basically good and harmonious. If we experience pain and distress, according to the healthy-minded, we simply need to adjust our mindset. A champion of this viewpoint is the mental healer who tells her patients, "there is nothing but Mind…as a man thinketh so is he."[27] Here, the evil and pain of the world exists only in our heads, and with proper instruction we can will them away.

James contrasted the healthy-minded with the "sick souls." For this type, the world and our lives within it are fundamentally flawed. All is not well and we stand in need of a basic change or radical cure. In spite of the nomenclature, the sick souls are in fact healthier than the healthy-minded. It's quite a burden for the healthy-minded to deny their suffering or suffer guilt for its eradicable presence. Try telling breast cancer patients that their suffering is self-created. To accept such counsel would be to suffer not only from disease but also from the impossible responsibility of curing the body without physical aid.

Most of us, unsurprisingly, would not be tempted to take or offer such advice in cases of chronic disease. Yet when we find ourselves addicted to work and schedule-induced frenzy, we routinely tell ourselves that a little yoga or meditation (or martinis or valium) can deter damage to our bodies and souls. One website claims that health arrives by renaming our frenzied lives "intentionally full" or "resplendent." I want in no way to depreciate or treat lightly the pain of those with crippling diseases, whether physical or mental. Rather, I seek to identify a new disease—one of epidemic proportions. It is the disease of hyper-busyness; its cause is anomic drivenness; and it is not subject to facile remedies.

It may sound like I, too, am offering easy solutions. "Just say 'no' to overwork" is not a particularly thoughtful or helpful mantra. Simplifying our lives means undoing countless habits and resisting prevailing customs—struggling against the powers of the age, really. Complicating our lives is all too human; simplifying them is the work of gods. It would entail a long—perhaps lifelong—process of incremental gains, frequent setbacks, and uncertainty about how to proceed. There would be many personal, practical questions: Will a new phone simplify or complicate my life? Is it wiser to hire someone to rake my leaves and plough my driveway or do it myself and save the money? Do I decline a job promotion that pays more but would require more hours at work and a longer commute? In the name of simplicity, do I refuse to participate in community groups concerned with housing for low-income families, shelter for the battered, environmentally sound development for my city? There exist a few guaranteed timesaving devices such as turning off the phone, Internet, or TV. Other than these, there is little that is simple about this process. Simplicity is a complicated task.

About a year before my crisis, I wrote the following letter to nine-year-old Laurel, one of the Walker children, with whom I had begun a correspondence:

> Poughkeepsie, 11 October
>
> Dear Laurel,
>
> I am sitting in my backyard on a fine autumn day. The leaves display the full spectrum of our northeast fall colors—everything from the deep green of the Norwegian maples, still yet to turn, to the bright red of the dogwoods and sugar maples; the sun is bright and warm on my face, and the shadows are longish, for the sun is not climbing as high these days; the breeze stirs my hair as I enjoy watching my chickens nap in the sun. The turkeys are visiting me and—I kid you not—insist on pecking at my laptop keyboard. The honeybees fly near me and appear anxious: as we approach winter, they are acting a bit frantic, searching for the last nectar.

Why do I often start my letters to you with descriptions of my daily, morning ritual—reading and writing in my backyard as my chickens and turkeys forage and nap? Perhaps because in my backyard, when I am doing my work and enjoying the beauty of nature around me, I feel especially at home—at ease—in the world. And then I think of other things and people that make me feel at home—like you and your family.

The Walkers are a good distraction for me. I know that sounds like a horrible thing to call dear friends, "a good distraction." But I assure you a distraction can be a very good thing. A couple of days ago, for instance, I was sitting by the wood stove, it was beautiful and cold out, and I was fretting about all the Vassar work I needed to do and was trying to race through it, when something caught my attention. Something was waving to me, as if to say: "Mark! Over here! Hi!" I looked up and the leaves—hundreds of them—were waving. Well, I couldn't resist. I waved back. First to the right to the hickory trees; then to the left to the maple trees; and then straight ahead to the great white oak. I felt better after waving. And I felt better still when I went out and visited the trees and chopped up some of their dead cousins. I knew they wouldn't mind. Indeed, they cheered me on. "Come out and join us, Mark, spend time with our kind." I could hear them, Laurel, really I could.

Like the trees, you and your family distract me: you help me think about and remember and do important things. And when I do the important things—like tend to my wood and to write letters to good friends—I do everything better, like my Vassar work (which can also be important). Laurel, in case I forget, will you thank your family for being a good distraction for me? In case I forget, I thank you now for helping me to remember the important things.

Love, Mark

Another great temptation is to put off simplification. We tell ourselves, *I'll slow down later*—after I pass my exams, graduate, land that job, get that promotion, buy that house, put the kids through college, retire. After I die. The commercial market responds to our addiction to overwork by prescribing timesaving devices and measures supposedly engineered to mitigate our frenzy and bring us closer to perfection.

None of these comes with the warning: "Increased efficiency may be hazardous to your mental and physical health." The danger lies not with any single timesaver, any one shortcut. Rather, the risk is their accrual by a life and a culture obsessed with maximizing performance. As each task takes less time, we multiply the number of tasks for which we feel responsible. Our hectic pace renders us unable to give sufficient care to, or draw meaning from, our work. And while we dash through our lives, we lose sight of good work: work that is both useful and beautiful, that honors both nature and culture.

Some helpful, if paradoxical, counsel goes like this: *Citizens, if you want more time in your life, do things the slow way.* If you have an especially busy week, try to walk to work instead of driving; cook an elaborate meal instead of buying prepared food; make plans with friends instead of staying overtime in the office. The idea is that by slowing down, we will perceive and experience more time. Will we be as efficient and accomplish as much? Probably not. Will we do what needs to be done with more grace and excellence? Yes, and with pleasure.

Deirdre used to practice phlebotomy, the art of drawing blood, on oranges. After she earned her MA in biology, she decided to become certified as a clinical lab technician instead of going on for a PhD. To her, this path seemed more practical and less painful. Yet for someone as sensitive and gentle as Deirdre, phlebotomy, the direction her med-tech teachers steered her in, was far from painless. She would spend hours with those oranges: donning latex-free gloves, tightening a tourniquet around the center of the orange, speaking softly to the orange as she gently tapped its bumpy skin and inserted a small needle, drawing the pale juice through the tube and into the vial. She was determined to master this art. But while she was patient and compassionate—important qualities for the phlebotomist—Deirdre was anxious around people and their spidery, elusive veins. No matter how many oranges she punctured, she struggled to reliably draw human blood.

It was about 4:00 a.m. when she got the call. A local hospital needed her to come in and draw blood from a patient. It did not go well. She made five attempts, "sticking" the patient in the arm, the hand, and the forehead. Eventually an on-call physician begrudgingly but successfully drew the blood. The dawn light exposed her tear-stained face when she returned home. We hugged and reclined on a futon as she told me the events of the night. She felt like an utter failure. "It's okay," I reassured, "those must have been some tough, buried veins." "Yet *she* could do it," she replied, "and *you* probably could have done it. But me? What can *I* do?" There was nothing I could say. I tightened my arms around her body.

For a long time we held each other as the dawn pulled back the darkness. Then, without warning, Deirdre jumped up, strode to the kitchen, and gathered her oranges. I still remember the sharp citrus scent in the kitchen as she plied her needle. The sky was by now splashed with pink. I made us coffee.

In Stacey's coffee shop, Paul and I sipped our coffee, ate our lunch, and conversed as if we had all day. In truth, we had two hours, usually on a Tuesday. In time, we had learned to enter that restorative, hundred-and-twenty-minute space swiftly and then inhabit it leisurely. The strain and stress of our lives usually stayed outside our small table, the contemplative island from which we viewed the wide world—and our miniscule lives in it—dispassionately. Achieving equanimity in the face of high demands was a frequent topic of conversation. Practical headway was made not so much by discursive discoveries as by the very act of participating in the weekly ritual, our liturgical luncheon. The rite became so precious that we coordinated our teaching schedules a year in advance to secure the weekly reunion. No administrative meeting, no medical appointment, no publication deadline thwarted our lunch for over ten years.

We cultivated an ethos, an atmosphere in which we could breathe deeply, experience stillness and alertness, and consider life's challenges, blessings, and mysteries. After a few years, we established the clandestine *Cladis-Kane Center for Speculative Inquiry* devoted to these very principles: conversation, contemplation, and slowing down. In time, the Center would win grants, such as the one that funded our Southwest trip, cross-list its courses at Vassar, and induct four or five qualified Vassar graduates as Fellows each May. We had, in effect, created a shadow department—*the Department of Gnosis,* with its own faculty, set of courses, and major—that operated covertly on the Vassar College campus. Years later when Stacey sold her restaurant, she insisted on a clause in the contract: *The small bronze plaque, "The Cladis-Kane Center for Speculative Inquiry," shall under no circumstances be removed from the east wall.* And to this day the plaque remains, appropriately hidden behind a large cooler.

What the Walkers facilitated via their children, chickens, and community dances—namely, lessons in slowing down and remembering the important things in life—the Center nurtured via reflective communion and genial friendship. And both the Walkers and the Center started to influence my scholarship and teaching. My intellectual loves, as it turned out, shined more brightly (and brought more joy) as I slowed down, worked the land, held the child's hand, and explored with Paul basic questions about the very nature and purpose of scholarship and teaching.

❧

As I have said, different kinds of pain come from over- and under-working. As an educator in search of a course, I've noticed how students in residential colleges are sheltered to a great extent from menial or manual work—work that could bring daily opportunities for significant learning and health. I have in mind such tasks as cooking meals, cleaning rooms, or raking leaves. Keeping students from humdrum chores is supposed to be a good thing—we wish to protect them from dull adult life. We treat our students thus as Disembodied Minds. Everything is arranged so they can read and write and think with efficiency, so they can be unburdened by the tasks of Embodied Living (save, perhaps, the treadmill workouts at the college gym). In the process, we shelter them from opportunities for spiritual and emotional maturation. We deny them, for example, the experience of dishwashing as a form of thanksgiving: there are dishes to wash because there is food to eat. Each plate, fork, spoon, and cup is an object to be treated mindfully; each can teach care and attention. And if a student learns to wash a bowl with great care, she can develop the capacity to read a sentence with attention.

As a result of this artificial, concentrated, disembodied existence, students suffer and, like everyone else, seek their own intense form of escape or recreation. Their lives often vacillate between strenuous, hectic study time and excessive, hazardous party time. These modes of existence exact a heavy toll. Student Counseling Services cannot keep up with the increase in cases of depression, anxiety, and eating disorders. Additionally, the adults in these students' lives submit to their own form of manic, disembodied living, and so provide little direction as role models. Our culture has invested enormous energy to liberate us from tasks that require our bodies. Yet could it be that our liberation from bodily labor has not delivered us from grief but put us instead in a different kind of cage?

This all sounds gloomy, I know. I certainly don't want to do my laundry on a washboard, cook on a woodstove, or walk all day for a sack of flour. Nor do I want to give up my email account or stop texting and streaming movies. I do, however, want to take stock of cultural trends and developments and think about how to mitigate those that are less than or ambiguously desirable.

There are models that can offer help. We have exemplars of hopeful lifestyles—not the lives of the rich and famous, but those lives engaged in good work, simplicity, bodily health, and meaningful sociability. The Walkers and Paul offered me considerable help. But I looked also to more public, renowned exemplars. The final chapter in Helen and Scott Nearing's *Maple Sugar Book* is titled, "A Life as well as a Living." In it, the Nearings reflect on the relation between the art of sugaring and the art of living:

> We wanted to make a living in about half of our working time—say four or five hours a day—so that we would be freed from the livelihood problem and enabled to devote the other half of our time to study, teaching, writing, music, travel.[28]

This is a deeply humane value. It presents a profound challenge to our personal lives and also to the global market economy. By making do with less—by escaping the quagmire of consumer culture—the Nearings lived without debt, worked less, and presumably enjoyed more. Indeed, they possessed more. They held time—time for quiet contemplation, social engagement, education, art, and travel. They adopted what they called the daily 4-4-4 formula: "four hours for bread labor, four hours for vocation [i.e., reading and writing], and four hours for social intercourse." This principle incites my fear, hope, and longing. It threatens my identity as one whose self-worth derives from productivity in my career. It offers freedom from that prodigious burden, "I am what I produce."

This lifestyle also poses a radical challenge to our extractive global economy. If we worked less we would buy and borrow less, which, in effect, would put a break on those global engines that would have us produce, consume, and pollute more. It would arrest, by gentle neglect, rapacious practices that threaten social and natural habitats around the globe. Could the world's populations survive a massive drop in global GDP? Can we survive without such measures?

I understand the Nearings' principle is by many accounts unrealistic. Could all individuals or families opt out of consumerism, debt, and rampant careerism? Would we want to? Could global economies survive such simplicity? Yet how realistic is the prevailing belief that our current way of life is sustainable, with its overconsumption and overproduction, with its laborious toll on love and life? We need alternatives. We can't, of course, all head to Vermont with the Nearings and practice sugaring. Yet standing for a moment and attending to alternative patterns of life can help us take steps that might promote our own joy, meaning, and health.

So, there I was at Shiprock, having worked with two wise and generous teachers in the desert, trying to comprehend the interrelation—the echo—between inner and outer landscapes. What could possibly set me and my remedies apart from the self-help industry that I've been critiquing? After all, I was in the land of New Age pilgrimage, trying out various "contemplative techniques." By any lights, I must have appeared a crunchy devotee with a likely library of self-help books and a worn copy of *Spirituality for Dummies.*

Perhaps my earlier criticism of the self-help industry sounded too unsympathetic or glib. Yes, a market has responded to the spiritlessness of the age. And what after all is this market—this vast tapestry of producers, sellers, and buyers—but various flesh-and-blood individuals struggling to get through the day in the face of suffering? At least those in the self-help and "Mind, Body, Spirit" industries have responded to these difficult times by offering products they believe may bring health and wholeness. In the process, they hope to make an okay living, to bring home a decent salary. Farmers nourish our bodies and deserve a fair wage; why not the same for those trying to feed our famished hearts?

Not long ago at a street fair I saw grace for sale. That's right—*grace*. It was in a little blue atomizer. I never did learn its exact ingredients, although I'm fairly certain lavender was present and perhaps some lemongrass (the listed ingredients were "vibrational essences of Gemini, Sagittarius, Pisces Full Moons and Spring Equinox"). The vendor offered me a sample. She sprayed some grace over me and asked how I felt. I answered honestly. I felt a little tingly all over, my nose started to itch, and I became somewhat calm. Not a spiritually nuanced reply, I know, but I have little experience in the way of bottled virtues. Later, however, the small print on the bottle helped me sort out my experience: "GRACE: For Grateful Acceptance of Self." Ah, so *that's* what I felt—the sensation of self-acceptance. What, I wonder, would I have experienced had I read, "SPITE: For Spiritless Indulgence of the Ego"? In any case, I felt a little better having been misted. And I would have bought this product for $8.50 had not the vender, probably out of pity for my haplessness, offered it to me for free.

There I was, then, a college professor with a PhD from Princeton and a post-doc from Stanford, ready to purchase a little blue bottle of grace. Most of us have needs—vast, cavernous needs—that demand some satisfaction by any medley of methods and means. And some venders have raced in to meet those needs. I can't say I blame them. Bottling and selling grace is more benign than bottling and selling vodka or gin. Still, it makes me wonder. Given the dimensions of what ails us, that great cavity in our chest, is it wise to let an aerosol spray absorb the responsibility of facing and transforming our lives? I enjoy vodka and gin, yet I must not turn to them for help, for my pain demands a stronger, more difficult route to dissolution. Grace in a bottle is simply too easy. It dissipates too quickly. I am left with an itchy nose, a heavy heart.

Such curatives remind me of the former practice of selling indulgences, the infamous fundraising initiative of the Roman Catholic Church. At its worst, it exploited people's fears and needs. They were anxious, and a product—an indulgence—was marketed to comfort them. *Buy a little grace.* We buy grace all the time, in a good bottle of wine, a meal out, a movie, a vacation. Blaise Pascal cautioned us against the temptation of averting attention away from ourselves by filling our lives with distractions. Yet I suspect that his warning about *divertissement* applies mainly to those who regularly live outside themselves. Achieving temporary relief from our selves—from pressing personal concerns—by means of an indulgence in the form of some pleasure and respite—should not be shunned. There are all kinds of retreats. A retreat, however, is not a place to dwell.

When diversion becomes a way of life and a principle means of coping, we have to work harder and harder to achieve any comfort. If one drink per day worked last year, we'll need two next year. If a vacation to Maine satisfied us last fall, we may need to travel to Singapore this spring. The diversions incessantly grow in size, number, and combination. All the while our lives—our character, maturation, and self-knowledge—undergo neglect. One day we will have to return home to ourselves. And when we do, we may find our lives in disrepair. It will be a difficult homecoming.

Were the Walkers, then, a diversion from my life? Were my chickens? A few months before the crisis, I wrote in my journal about two of my hens, Luisa and Lorenza:

> As Luisa patiently sits in the nesting box, focused on laying her morning egg, I make my cooing sound to Lorenza and she flies up to the deck to join me. Soon, she is fast asleep next to me in the sun. Do I derive too much pleasure, too

> much emotional sustenance from a sleeping chicken? After all, Lorenza is a chicken. Are there no limits to the human craving for love, or to how we find or create that love?

Looking back, I see myself again and again asking the question, "Where am I to find love?" "The soul knows for certain only that it is hungry," Simone Weil noted.[29] I remember when seven-year-old Mary-Claire Walker handed me my Valentine's Day card. Excitedly, I tore open the envelope and found a lovely painted card with her child's lettering, "I love *everyone*! Happy Valentine's Day." I was sorely disappointed. I admit it: I wanted to be that "special person" in someone's life. And I was, of course. In Paul, the Walkers, and, yes, my chickens, I experienced affection and comfort. But their presence revealed an absence in my marriage. "The important thing," Simone Weil continued, "is that [the soul] announces its hunger by crying.... The danger is not lest the soul should doubt whether there is any bread, but lest, by a lie, it should persuade itself that it is not hungry."

Perhaps earlier in the marriage I had persuaded myself that I was not hungry and that all was well, but that prevarication was becoming less and less convincing. The evidence was mounting—I was ravenous. About a year before the crisis, for example, Deidre had decided to stay home rather than join me for an all-expense-paid residency at the Rockefeller Foundation's Bellagio Center. The center, affectionately known as Villa Serbelloni, is a seventeenth-century estate built on a wooded promontory just above Lake Como in the foothills of the Italian Alps. Surrounded by fifty acres of lush parks and tremendous mountains ascending out of the lake, the center is unquestionably one of the most stunning places in the world. Understanding as much, Deidre still declined to join me.

Even so, I can't say I blamed her. The center is the *scholar's* paradisiacal garden. Every meal, every break, every evening is dominated by erudite, highbrow conversation. That prospect can appear daunting and tiresome to a nonacademic, even one as bright and studious as Deirdre. Noting her prized "alone time," she stayed home. My journal entries at Bellagio are marked by the presence and absence of beauty:

> Yesterday at dusk I climbed the promontory up to the old ruined castle. All was quiet, except for the rush of the wind and the distant sound of waves purring against the shores of Lake Como. It occurred to me that not only was I writing about Rousseau's private path—the way of the Solitary Walker—but that I was on that path. But once I reached the top of the promontory an apprehension haunted me: my solitude is also loneliness. The face is hidden from me. I used to gaze into it, healed by its beauty and presence. Now, even if facing me, her look is vacant, distant, impassive.

Warning signs? Who can say? I believed her accounts of her depression and trusted that, if she was hiding something from me, it did not pertain to our marriage. It was private. It would be dealt with and the face of love would then return.

While at Shiprock, Paul and I went in search of a poem. Paul had first visited Shiprock a few years prior, and on that occasion, he climbed up high, wrote a poem, and inserted it in a small crevice above a narrow ledge. Later he recited the poem at one of our weekly lunches. As it was almost my birthday, I asked him to write the poem down for me. Inscribed on a paper napkin, "Lines Left at Shiprock" now hangs framed in my office.

> Westward, wings of rock
> enfold the setting sun
> as the world tilts
> towards the edge of night.

You have come this far
and still you think
your life will endure.[30]

What endures? We talk about enduring friendships, marriages, and memories. We talk about enduring pain. Then we visit a place like Shiprock, a place that ages not in years or decades but in millennia, in eons. It makes you wonder, what endures? Sometimes, I am swept by a bracing breeze and awoken to the reality of my nature, the particle of my body among numberless particles borne on vast winds of time and space. Shiprock sweeps, too. It sweeps us off the orbit of our selves, our egocentric circuit, our doctrine of the Enduring Self, and thereby blunts our pain. For it is painful to cling to a self forever clinging to its pain.

What endures? Even the millennia of Shiprock are numbered. Days and nights—their number, too, is finite. The sun will fail to rise someday. Yet there will remain the question of those particles—those bits and pieces of Shiprock and sun and everything between, including your body, my body. What endures? Not my worries or fears or desires or achievements. No legacy, no pain. But what of those particles? What of our love? I am less sure of what might endure than of what must vanish.

And a poem—what is its longevity? How long can "Lines Left at Shiprock" survive? Paul and I wanted to find out, so we searched for the poem. We had our doubts. It had been five years since he wrote the poem and placed it in one of Shiprock's hundred million crevices. And even if we did find it, would the poem be intact?

It was not an easy climb. The rock was dangerous. I have had some rock climbing experience, and my first climbing instructor had drilled into me the lesson, "trust the rock." But this limestone felt untrustworthy. As Paul remarked as we clambered up the crumbling stone, "Don't take anything for granite." And the rock was not the only hazard. During the climb I realized that Paul, too, is dangerous. He is not a tame poet. I have said with complete certitude that Paul Kane is the most thoughtful, sensitive, and mild-mannered person I have ever known. That holds true. But this gentle man alarmed me as I trailed him up the escarpment, searching for the route he had once traveled alone, the way that led to the poem.

Why does it surprise me that Paul the Gentle, the giver of comfort, is also Paul the Risk-Taker? Perhaps there is a connection. Perhaps the inner confidence that makes possible a spirit of generosity, acceptance, and kindness can be, too, a source of strength and daring. Climbing a mountain is like piloting a life. We encounter obstacles and quandaries, note if there is a simple way out, and yet embrace the more difficult route if that is what is required. Regardless of the route, self-possession, skill, and hope must lead.

We found the poem. During our climb we had joked about the possibility of discovering that the poem had been marked up in red by an anonymous reader with the final comment, "best work to date," followed by the letter grade, B–. No joking took place, however, when we pulled it finally from the thin fissure that for five years had enfolded and sheltered the poem. Quietly we retrieved "Lines Left at Shiprock," read it to ourselves, and stood in silence. In that silence I felt held and sheltered by something greater than myself, greater even than those wings of rock around me. In that moment, I surrendered.

You can lose and find a poem. But how about a life? Can you lose your life and then recover it—just as it was? Or must you surrender one life to gain another? During my marriage, I didn't know I was dying. I did know that the life I had was not the one I was seeking. I met the stillness, silence, and disengagement in my marriage with a growing desire for motion, voice, and a sense of commitment. Again, I hear this longing in old journal entries:

> I want to be encumbered. I want those angora rabbits. I want to be held by the necessity of feeding them. I want the chickens, the bees, the turkeys, the wood to chop, friends to love, and children. Yes, I want children—to feed and clothe and care for. I want to be encumbered.

It never occurred to me that the loss of my marriage was waiting for me on my path. Such a death was unthinkable. I suppose I assumed that my marriage would mature and become more robust, or else that I would find other sources—such as the Walkers and Paul—of love and growth. Percy Shelley wrote of Wordsworth, "thou hast wept to know / That things depart which never may return."[31] But not knowing of final departures, I could not yet weep. The deaths that I knew were of a different kind, as recorded in this journal passage written four days before my crisis:

> 31 July
> After I slaughter a rooster it's good to gather the feathers and bring them inside. This way, I remember the beauty of the bird. I mourn the life I will never again hold. I surrender to the inescapable: life requires death.

I was certainly not the first to surrender in the face of a mountain. Percy Shelley did it. At the foot of Mont Blanc, the agnostic poet caught religion—or was caught by it. The religious devotion Mont Blanc commanded was not the conservative Christianity of Shelley's day. Rather, the Mountain religion asked that he listen to its mysteries without regard to expedient religious and political "codes"—all those doctrines and dogmas, laws and decrees, that attempt to systemize the divine and subject humans to its arbitrary, often cruel, authority:

> The wilderness has a mysterious tongue
> Which teaches awful doubt, or faith so mild,
> So solemn, so serene, that man may be,

But for such faith, with nature reconciled;
Thou has a voice, great Mountain, to repeal
Large codes of fraud and woe....[32]

The Mountain teaches humility and "awful doubt" (receptiveness to awe and wonder) by its glacial challenge to human pride and hubristic religion. "Faith so mild," it turns out, is our best chance at reconciliation not only with nature but with each other, for the voice of the Mountain has the power to humble the proud and to reform fraudulent laws and institutions.

The Mountain, then, is a powerful teacher, but the student—in this case Shelley—has his own power, too. This is always the case in effective education. Power must not rest in the educator alone; the student is not a mere vessel waiting to be filled. And so the poem, "Mont Blanc," ends by affirming not only the humbling power of the Mountain-Teacher, but also the indispensable and active role of the student:

And what were thou [Mont Blanc], and earth, and stars,
  and sea,
If to the human mind's imaginings
Silence and solitude were vacancy?

Evidently, even lessons in humility require the active and expansive imagination of Shelley as student. Mont Blanc—and the earth and stars and sea!—cannot speak or teach without the active consent or engaged presence of the pupil. Shelley, like William Clift, had a conversation with a mountain, and once again the human's role was as learner. But listening can be active and imaginative—it *must* be if we are to hear or learn something new.

Of course, Shiprock and Mont Blanc are no ordinary teachers. If we speak little before them, it is because they take our breath away. How much can we say to the "sound no other sound can tame?" We offer our imagination and reasoning, but in the end we receive the gift of our own surrender in the face of the infinite.

Shelley left Mont Blanc with a sense of having been healed. What healing comes from severe confrontation with our limits and frailty? When we surrender to the powers of necessity—powers "remote" and "inaccessible"—we begin to learn something about acceptance and graciousness. We learn to accept our limits and to greet our own powers graciously. With the help of the Mountain, we are restored to a properly human measure in a profoundly therapeutic process. It is a priceless gift. Perhaps this is why, after leaving the Mountain, Percy the agnostic came to believe in a divinity that defied all names except that of Love.

Sometimes in the quiet of the night I would awaken and embrace Deirdre, firmly and tenderly, as if trying to hold together a delicate bundle of dried twigs. I think now that I was trying to hold *us* together, to tether myself to her lest we both collapse.

Loneliness occurs not only in the absence of others but also in the presence of the beloved—in this case, while she was sleeping. At night, I would wrestle with lions and serpents—dark fears and doubts. Deirdre's slumber often caused me to awaken. Accompanied by the hum of the refrigerator, the murmur of leaves in the wind, and Deirdre's rhythmic breathing, I was alert to the acute hunger and loneliness lodged in my chest.

Surrendering, as I was beginning to understand it, entails not only admission of inadequacy but acceptance of self. And acceptance of self requires love of self, which, in turn, requires some conviction or belief that the self is lovable and loved. Loved by what or by whom? Spirit? Life? God? Nature? Mystery? Whatever its name, I have come to believe in this source of love and acceptance. I believe that it is entirely trustworthy—trustworthy, but not necessarily *accommodating.* It will confront us and shake us. It will challenge our pettiness and fears that we might become, to a greater degree, people of generosity and courage. It will fracture our narrow sight that we might become people of vision.

The source of this self-love is not a substitute for any particular, contingent experience of love—the gaze of a lifelong companion, the child's delicate handhold, the healing conversation with a friend, the sweep of a breeze on a summer evening. Such particulars are *inherently* lovely. Such particulars are necessary for self-love. They belong to the source of love and flow to and from it. They are not, however, always sufficient. For there are times in our lives when the particulars of love seem to fail us, and in those dark times we need to know, or at least believe, that we are held by something like Love itself. This profession, I know, is controversial. I do not write with the authority of a theologian. Yet as a professor, here, now, on this one topic, I desire to profess. For I have become convinced of the necessity of believing in this Love (even as loath as I am to try to *argue* anyone into this belief).

There is a relation between self-acceptance and self-transformation. Moral and spiritual maturation, I have said, require that we recognize that all is not well within the self and that we need to work on this self. Acknowledging the need for change, in other words, is part of the process of growth. Now, however, I am adding self-acceptance as another basic condition for becoming more fully human.

The cosmetic and fashion industries have correctly identified two deep-seated desires within us: the longing to be loved and the longing to be worthy of that love. These industries would have us believe that our longing to be loved can only be satisfied *after* we do the hard work of becoming worthy of love. Acceptance of self, in other words, arrives only upon having made the self acceptable—through a daily, ritualistic diet and exercise regime and the application of beauty products. Yet by placing self-transformation before self-acceptance, these industries have made nearly impossible the satisfaction of either desire. This satisfaction requires, in fact, a priority in direct opposition to what these industries would have us believe. Primacy should be placed on self-acceptance; that is to say, *self-acceptance precedes the possibility of self-transformation.* Although these two longings are closely related, acceptance of self is a condition for transformation of self. Too often, our consumer culture reverses this order.

I am not suggesting a simple hierarchal relation between self-acceptance and self-transformation, as if we first achieve the one and then move cleanly and subsequently to the other. Both require constant attention. A dance—a dialectical relation—keeps the two in motion: self-acceptance encourages the work of transforming the self; and self-transformation, in turn, fortifies the capacity to accept the self. Yet in this dance, self-acceptance takes the lead. We need to accept ourselves as we are if we are to work on changing and bettering ourselves. We need to find ourselves lovable and loved if we are to sustain the work of maturation in love.

In what may be my earliest memory, I am calling out for my mother. Alone in my room, on top of a blue comforter dotted with sailboats and anchors, I am panicking as I call out for my mother's face. When do we stop calling? What happens when we bring that cry into a marriage, as a grown man or woman? Not the cry for our mothers, but for the face of love that sustains us when we fall, when we are unsure, when we are weary. Is it shameful to try to marry that face? Is it better, more mature, to marry someone whom we know will *not* be that face for us, thereby dodging exposure and dependency?

False choices. As adults, we seek the faces that facilitate our independence but also accept our neediness and vulnerability. We seek interdependency and reciprocity. Yet we also suffer from a form of denial. We often refuse to admit the depth of our vulnerability and our need for caring attention. In human relationships—not to mention our relation to the non-human world—our dependence nearly always exceeds our independence. As long as we continue to seek the face of love, we are needy. Yet we do not become less vulnerable upon finding this face; rather, we must then meet the task of accepting our dependence with grace and trust, empowered by our love.

Grace precedes will—the gift before the effort of love—even if both are necessary. So we begin in grace. We begin with the belief that we are loved unconditionally by someone or something—by Spirit or Nature, or by parent, partner, or friend who can approximate unconditional love. Maintaining this belief at all times is virtually impossible. Yet if we are to work on ourselves, there must be present at least the seed of conviction that we are lovable and acceptable now, in this moment, as we are.

Acceptance of pain, especially emotional pain, is one of the most difficult steps to self-acceptance. Affliction can assault self-worth. If I regard my suffering as unnatural (and we often do), I will blame myself—my weak will or poor judgment or thin skin. I will tell myself, "I never should have allowed myself to be so vulnerable"; "I never should have entered that relationship"; "I never should have taken that job." To utter such regret is to wish for another self, place, or vocation. To escape pain, I long to escape myself and my circumstances; I tell myself my suffering is an indicator of unworthiness, weakness, and insufficiency as I stand.

There is also the seemingly opposite response. This is to decry always the experience of pain as the unmitigated fault of something or someone outside the self—the completely absolved, utterly victimized self. In this case, the pain considered as unnatural is in direct proportion to an immoderate sense of pride. The distended, delicate ego is forever experiencing offense, and sources of distress—and there are many for this person—are met with outrage.

This person, however, is not in fact so different from the one who blames her- or himself. Both strain to construct a world-view that seems to deny the necessity of pain. Yet learning to accept myself, which is necessary to transform myself, entails learning to accept my pain. And acceptance of pain requires that I stop deeming it unnatural. It is not an intruder in this life, threatening to rob me of all that is dear. It need not startle or surprise. On the contrary, my daily expectation should be that pain of some ilk is likely to visit me. Its presence is not an indication of my own inner weakness or of an especially antagonistic world. When pain comes my way, I do not want to admonish myself or those around me. Rather, I want to accept that distress in some form occurs when we are engaged in life. To dodge it would require that I evade life, that I stop breathing. For pain is as natural as breath, and to blame myself for the experience of pain is to blame myself for being alive.

Keep your mind in hell, and despair not. These words of St. Silouan of Mt. Athos have haunted me ever since I first read them.[33] I don't pretend to have grasped their entire meaning, if there is such a thing. But I often find myself contemplating the phrase. "Keep your mind in hell." This suggests to me that it is vitally important for us to acknowledge the difficulties of existence, for us to extirpate illusions of an easy life. Life is risky and often painful, and to attempt to deny *this* is likely to cause us all the more pain. To "keep your mind in hell" is to admit to yourself that life poses difficulties to be coped with daily.

Yet what about the second part, "and despair not"? If not for this, St. Silouan would be simply a grim realist. But he adds, *despair not,* thereby becoming a person of hope. Yet his is not easy hope or wishful thinking. Rather, the words come to us as a somber imperative: despair not. St. Silouan charges us first to acknowledge our pain and next not to be crushed by it.

How are we to obey this dual command? I don't know all the ways. In St. Silouan's Eastern Orthodox tradition, love is a way;

in the German Hegelian tradition, humor is a way. Regardless, our ability to bear suffering comes not from self-aggrandizement and overconfidence in our power to endure, but in the constant back-and-forth between our *will* to love and laugh and the *grace* to do so as we struggle in hell, where we are most tempted to neglect love and laughter. Keep your mind in hell: accept that life is often like this. But despair not: practice love and laughter in grace.

There are of course types of pain that are unacceptable, unnatural, and rightly startling. This is why we do not—or should not—tolerate abusive relationships, torture, or humiliation. Consenting to such inflictions leads not to self-acceptance but to self-disfigurement. There exist plenty of kinds of unacceptable pain that we should shun: a child becomes sick from pesticides; an employee is fired by dishonest management; a student is hospitalized due to hazing. And then there are all those cases too difficult to judge, because the line between acceptable and unacceptable pain is unclear. Still, a logic remains: when we accept an instance of necessary pain, we thereby accept it as an instance of life, and the assignment of blame is no longer the dominant preoccupation. When, on the other hand, we judge the pain as unacceptable, we deem it not a natural feature of life, but a thing akin to evil, and assignment of blame and responsibility becomes a moral imperative.

Self-acceptance and concomitant pain-acceptance have nothing to do with complacency. In order to accept ourselves we have to know *what* we are accepting, and such honest self-knowledge is difficult and disturbing, and tends toward humility. Self-acceptance, then, requires seeing ourselves truthfully—seeing with something like impartiality or objectivity. This, then, is another reason that self-acceptance, which includes knowledge of our profound limits, can occasion human transformation: it opposes all forms of self-satisfaction and smugness. It will not brook complacency.

❧

Days before my crisis, Deirdre and I ate at a Chinese buffet in a Poughkeepsie strip mall on Route 9. Later that day, Deirdre would catch a plane for Minneapolis, and, over our dinner of fruit, dumplings, and sesame noodles, I tried to make conversation about her upcoming trip. Her emerald eyes kept mostly to her plate as she provided terse replies. My eyes eventually turned from Deirdre to the table behind her, where an overweight middle-aged man sat alone, eating from a heaping plastic plate. I pitied him. Facilely, I diagnosed the situation: eating was the mechanism by which this man coped with loneliness.

When I remember this day, I am struck by my own staggering arrogance. I knew nothing of this man's life. I knew nothing of my *own* life, of what was to become of it. Within a week, I would be hiding, sobbing, in a dark garage; I would be throwing midnight stones at Jeff and Kathy Walker's bedroom window, desperate for comfort. Looking away from my table and life, I judged the large man in the Chinese restaurant. I wonder now what he would have seen had he looked at me?

"Contemplation is no pain-killer."[34] When Thomas Merton wrote that line, he knew of what he wrote. In his lifetime he contemplated and suffered much, often at the same time. I read that line this morning and found myself wishing I had read it earlier. It explains my initial and perhaps abiding failure as a contemplative. For I had turned to contemplation to ease my pain, not to stir it up and to contend with it. Evidently, I collaborate with a culture that goes to great lengths to escape pain. I, too, carry the unnatural burden of attempting to escape the inescapable.

With "Lines Left at Shiprock" at Paul's side, we stood high on the mountain in that moment of surrender. I was enfolded by that seam of sky and rock—every part and moment, past and present, joyful and sad, wise and rash, willing and stubborn, caring and callous, reverent and glib. For a moment, the full depth of my personhood was quietly and unmistakably held.

In that time and place I glimpsed what it meant to admit pain and not be overwhelmed by it. *To consent to pain and still feel at home in the world.* An acceptance neither cheerful nor gloomy. Consistent happiness, I was beginning to understand, would not and could not be my lot. I must seek something else—not something less, but something different. A different course.

Deirdre returned from Minneapolis in early August on a Friday, a day after I had watched *The Perfect Storm* with my Vassar colleague. By Monday, most of the pieces of the puzzle had been put in place. What had I discovered? More than I can or should write of in these pages. Infidelity? Yes, but must details be disclosed? What of respect for her and the love we once shared? I will say the faithlessness was not a base or sleazy variety. Deirdre's infidelity was part of her search for an identity, a life, a place free from darkness and tears. For much time now, I learned, she had been plotting a way out of our marriage. Evidently, I was not the only one in the marriage who felt alone and desperate for life.

Beethoven's most tumultuous crescendos are often followed by his most delicate decrescendos. That was the progression of that Monday night. The crescendo began when I started to rip pictures out of the photo albums in the living room. Some albums were embroidered, others leather-bound, striped, or multicolored—yet they all comprised the same phony pictures: the unhappy couple feigning bliss. I felt mocked by the couple in the photos, grinning in their wedding clothes, posing insouciantly on a beach. No photos showed our tears, our anger, our torpidity.

I had hoped that shredding our treasured albums in front of Deirdre would have a pronounced effect on her—or at least *some* effect. I was disappointed: she watched impassively, unspeaking. I took it to the next level, uttering what I had thought unspeakable: "This marriage is over. It's a sham. We need to get a divorce." I stormed into the bedroom and collapsed on our bed. When she came in a while later, she asked only, "Will I get the car?" Her question was not calculated or cruel; it was entirely pragmatic. Lying on our bed, aching for emotional engagement, I realized suddenly that Deirdre had long been thinking about divorce, that she was by now so accustomed to the idea that her concerns were of a practical, logistical nature. "Will I get the car?" This sincere, inoffensive sentence cut me deeper than words of fury and hate.

Slowly, I repeated her question a few times aloud. I turned from her and peered into the open closet, staring at her clothes—the striped yellow shirt, the green lacy dress, the tattered straw hat with its limp red bow. I gazed at the intimacy and tenderness of my everyday life with Deirdre. I moaned, "No, no, no, no, no." When my anger turned to tears, Deirdre touched me, placing her soft hand on my shoulder. And so comfort came, and with it a fragile and protracted decrescendo that lasted for one and half years.

I believe that Deirdre was ready on that Monday night to accept the demise of the marriage. Yet when she saw my pain, my inability to acknowledge the inevitable, she would not independently perform the major surgery—the cutting into two what was once one.

Shortly after the storm sundered my life on that warm August evening, I read one of Paul's poems. While its title was "Acceptance," I read the poem with resentment and fear.

Acceptance

Gray across the bridge, the bridge
itself silver, shining in the dull air,

the gray mist and water below
pale, obscuring any view but

the prevalent neutrality. Gray, then,
with splashed color, lights moving

slowly, the bridge trafficking in
anonymous lives, sequestered worlds—

it could be this way always, somber
and yet not sad: washed, toned down,

quiet, even serene. It would be
all right, with much still to praise.[35]

The poem, it seemed, was admonishing me. It spoke of what my life had recently become—"dull air," "gray mist," "pale water." When I looked to the future, back then, I could see for myself no more than a "prevalent neutrality," a "washed, toned down" existence in my own sequestered, lonely world. Paul's poem confirmed this bleak future, adding, gently but firmly, that such a prospect "would be all right." It would be enough and "with much still to praise."

Yet I wanted so much more! The poem's Wordsworthian "lonely cheer" seemed to me too austere. It stung. I wanted supportive community, not "sequestered worlds." I wanted vibrant joy, not a life "toned down." I wanted love tender and yet ardent, not days "somber and yet not sad." Becoming satisfied with "not sad" was my fear and—I imagined—my destiny. Paul's poem, then, had named my fear, had declared my fate, had pinned me down on that page with his words.

I understand the poem differently now. It no longer seems altogether dreary, not with its shining silver bridge, moving lights, splashed color, and serenity—yes, much to praise. And as much could be said of my own life, which I have also begun to understand anew.

The greater interpretative shift, however, lies not in now noticing and counting the pleasant facets of the poem or of my life. The greater shift is not quantitative. Acceptance, in Paul's poem, is not about identifying our blessings, or being satisfied with less, or knowing when we have enough (although this talent is needed in our lives and culture). Acceptance, rather, is a graceful stance—a receptive disposition—toward every particular in our lives: every event, person, creature, or thing, that is present or notably missing. When we receive each particular in our lives as an impermanent gift, we can hold it gratefully and release it gracefully. Pain, too, can be held and released skillfully, although it requires great maturity and often hindsight to conceive of it as an impermanent gift.

Understood as such, acceptance is a discipline that requires daily application and cultivation. Although the capacity to accept may be most evident in cases of privation, it is also present in the face of plenty. It brings, then, not only the freedom to do without but also the freedom to receive gifts of health, romance, family, vocation, avocation, and friendship. To accept these goods appropriately is to respect their autonomy and their fragility: none belongs to us absolutely.

Paul's poem is about a way to experience life as "quiet, even serene." Of course, it is only one poem—that is, one meditation on one aspect of life. It is not the complete Gospel of St. Paul. Paul's gospel, if there is one, is made manifest in his everyday choices and actions, his ordinary and remarkable life—by whose example I began to learn about acceptance.

On that night when Deidre asked about the car, my life was anything but "quiet, even serene." The evening had decrescendoed insofar as I had stopped shredding photos and calling for divorce. But my life had been irreparably fractured. As I lay in bed listening to Deirdre's slumber and watching the clock shift past 2:00 a.m., I decided—or was compelled—to drive to the Walkers'. I was desperate for help, for emotional connection. Driving past all those sleeping homes, my life felt utterly alien to me, as if I was watching someone I had never met drive through the darkness to wake a sleeping family in the night. When I arrived at the Walkers' dark house, I decided not to knock on the door for fear of waking the children. Instead,

I found a stone and lobbed it at Kathy's and Jeff's window. I found another and another, until finally the bedroom light flicked on. Moments later, Jeff and Kathy were outside.

I had prepared an apology: "I know it's so late and I'm terribly sorry for waking you…." But when my eyes met theirs—eyes that had seen me hold their children, had seen me laugh in sunlight and firelight and starlight, had seen me haul their wood, feed their sheep, eat at their table—when I met those eyes that in all seasons had seen, known, and loved me, I turned from apology to entreaty. "Can you help me? My life has fallen apart. Can you help me?"

In Robert Frost's early poem, "Reluctance," he explores the sense of loss that comes with change—in particular, the transition from the season of flowers and warmth to that of fallen leaves and snow. Having climbed the "hills of view / And looked at the world," he declares matter-of-factly, "lo, it is ended. / The leaves are all dead on the ground, / Save those that the oak is keeping…." Though he seems to accept the loss stoically, the final stanza suggests otherwise:

> Ah, when to the heart of man
> Was it ever less than a treason
> To go with the drift of things,
> To yield with a grace to reason,
> And bow and accept the end
> Of a love or a season?[36]

Here, Frost reminds us of the worthy role of defiance in our lives. There is a place in the human heart for recalcitrance, for refusing to accept what is inexorable, for trying to keep a season or a love that can't be kept. It is difficult to imagine a sentiment more contrary to Zen or to my descriptions of Acceptance. Yet there it is: *reluctance*—veritable, arresting, and undeniable. Have I committed treason by endorsing acceptance? Have I been disloyal, as Frost might say, to the human heart?

The philosopher in me would like to offer some dialectic, some middle term, to reconcile Frost's "Reluctance" with Kane's "Acceptance." But I want to resist that urge. The human heart is big enough to hold both poems, both modes. We strive to practice acceptance; we frequently experience reluctance. This is who we are. To deny this is to betray the human heart. This condition—this humanity—we must *accept.*

I cannot fit the ways of acceptance and reluctance into a tidy system, yet with another poem by Frost, perhaps I can capture more truly their manner and tension. "The Road Not Taken" is one of those complex poems whose meaning is commonly reduced for easy handling or pedagogical relevance. Yesterday when I reread the poem, I was surprised by the novel experience its familiar words afforded. I always thought of the poem as a triumphant one, and would often hear, out of context, its most famous lines cited as an argument for self-determination.

> Two roads diverged in a wood, and I—
> I took the one less traveled by,
> And that made all the difference.[37]

In these words I had heard, "I, the hardy American, took the virgin path, the more challenging, the unpaved, and that heroism led to my success." But yesterday it struck me more as a poem about loss.

The first clue was the title. It is not "The Road Taken." Frost directs our attention not to the chosen way, but to the way *un*traveled, to what was left behind. "Two roads diverged in a yellow wood, / And sorry I could not travel both...." Here is not the boast of a trailblazer or headstrong pioneer. It is, rather, the sigh of one anticipating remorse or the experience of loss. For consolation, Frost tells himself he would keep the relinquished path "for another day!" But reality, inevitably, sets in: "Yet knowing how way leads on to way, / I doubted if I should ever come back." These words prepare us for the last stanza's prophetic gesture, "I shall be telling this with a sigh / Somewhere ages and ages hence..."

Both reluctance and acceptance have a place in "The Road Not Taken." Reluctantly, we must leave behind a path at the crossroads—a love, a job, a home, a belief. Like Frost, we may try to convince ourselves that loss can be avoided, that we can take both paths, perhaps at the same time. But in time we must make a decision. Back and forth we pace, debating and deliberating the way forward. Later we may tell ourselves the path we chose was the better way. This is natural. Yet, had the paths at the crossroads not been even—had they not been, on first sight, comparable—they would not have stopped us, or bade us linger in unquiet reflection. Frost initially justifies his chosen path as "having perhaps the better claim, / Because it was grassy and wanted wear." Yet, by the next line, he has already recanted: "Though as for that, the passing there / Had worn them really about the same."

A juncture of incommensurate paths of equal appeal—this is where Frost found himself, and this is where we have all been and will be again. At such junctures we would like to be decisive, confident, and in the end resolute. And some succeed in that. Yet for most of us, the heart, with its ways of attachment, longing, wonder, and imagination, does not let us proceed so easily. We suffer a little. We pay a toll at the crossroads. And that toll is often most expensive, not during the brooding and debating, but at the moment of our first step down the chosen path, the first step away from the forsaken path. For until then, both paths remain open. Both are paved with hope. Yet after the first step, while hope for the chosen path abides, hope for the other path quickly turns to mourning. There is no return. The step, like the tick of an atomic clock, is final. Everything is different now. "Way leads on to way."

Letting go of the forsaken or neglected path is the work of acceptance. Acknowledging that "way leads on to way," that we are borne today on the path we chose yesterday—this, too, is the work of acceptance.

Our movement toward acceptance is not usually linear. We

zigzag between acceptance and reluctance, between letting go and hanging on. If this motion is reminiscent of the movement of mourning, it is because this process, or procession, is itself a form of bereavement. In time, we increasingly rest near acceptance. Yet even long after the forsaken path is buried, it may resurface and bring with it an episode of grief. This is natural. This is human. This, too, is to be accepted. And someday we may say,

> Two roads diverged in a wood, and I—
> I took the one less traveled by,
> And that made all the difference.

We would not boast these lines. We would not shout them. We might utter them, like Frost, with a sigh. The mood of our speech could be unaffected, temperate, even chaste. And yet gratitude would have its place, as if to say,

> it could be this way always, somber
> and yet not sad: washed, toned down,
>
> quiet, even serene. It would be
> all right, with much still to praise.[38]

Here gratitude finds its voice in "Acceptance." Here Kane and Frost conspire to point the way to satisfaction and equanimity, a destination met regardless of paths chosen and neglected. This, too, is part of the search for a course. For some courses do not depend on one choice, one path, but on a deeper route that runs the length of our character and spirit.

In the months after I woke the Walkers in the night, I focused my time on Deirdre and on saving the marriage. While she was not indifferent to this salvage, Deirdre seemed to know what I refused to believe: that some paths must end, no matter how lovely their start, and that some loss, even great loss, cannot be fought. I had already departed down a different road.

Fifteen months later, I wrote in my journal:

> How to break brokenness? How to repair what is broken, split, splintered? When the pieces come apart, again and again, do you reattempt the surgery of repair? Or do you leave the pieces behind, saying to yourself, "Get up, broken heart; time to start anew?" How to break brokenness?

By now Deirdre and I had been living together as congenial roommates for over a year. Each time I was about to take a step toward embracing change and admitting that the marriage was over, I held myself back. Moving forward meant acknowledging that my old, familiar life had departed, and that change had already arrived. My pain was rooted in the old life but also in the uncertainty of the new.

High up on Shiprock Paul and I stood. Why were we there? There were the professional reasons—the team-taught course and Paul's book. There were personal reasons, too. I was there to learn how to bow and accept the end of a love. Convalesce in the Southwest. Lose myself in hope of finding myself, or something like that. Winged Rock—what better place to learn the ways of solidity and rest, buoyancy and flight? Winged Rock—with its steadiness, its wind-chiseled face, its broad wings folded for a centuries-long moment. Winged Rock—could this two-word poem describe a life?

I was searching for a shape: a well-defined structure for my life. But my search for order led to as much chaos. "Order is indeed the dream of man, but chaos, which is only another word for dumb, blind, witless chance, is still the law of nature."[39] Larry Morgan, a character in Wallace Stegner's novel, *Crossing to Safety*, is one of my heroes. When he spoke these lines, he was reflecting on his wife's contraction of polio, an event that altered irrevocably their life together. Chaos dismembered order. Dreams were first postponed, then curtailed; their aspirations took the shape of meals, baths, trips to the bathroom.

It sounds grim. The narrative of *Crossing to Safety* never once departs from the daily, the ordinary, the routine. And when the polio arrives, the concrete, quotidian details of disease bear down especially hard on the reader, making deep impressions. Still, the novel is not bleak. Witless chance may be the law of nature, but Sally and Larry Morgan's response to it was neither witless nor random. A steady, reciprocal love—I don't know what else to call it—elevated their shared lives, not up and out of disease, but certainly out of despair. They learned to negotiate the basics, to celebrate small victories, and to expect chaos. They became more—more fully themselves, more fully human—than they would have on a smoother path.

Chaos may be the law of nature, and like everything else, our encounters with chaos contribute to the shape of our lives. But we do not have to let this chaos define us. And we can cross to safety—safety not as shelter from chaos, but safety as the presence of love in its midst.

I believe in crossings to safety. I have now traveled them with some frequency. I have now experienced love in the throes of chaos. In death alone can we evade chaos, or perhaps in lives as still and sheltered as buried corpses. Otherwise, chaos is always there—outside us, in a virus heading our way; inside us, in a disturbing memory. It is not the enemy. Neither is it a friend. It is no more benign or malevolent than the tornado that spares this house and destroys that one. Chaos is disinterested necessity.

In the Southwest I searched for order and found chaos. The rock gave way; the teachers raised questions; the turmoil within me clamored loudly in the quiet desert. As loath as I am to admit it, and as cautious as I'd be to speak it to a friend in tumult, I must report what I have learned: *from chaos emerges the possibility of re-creation.* Of new life. It's a well-known process: to be strengthened, some bones must be broken and reset. Still, no one I know wants a fractured femur. We reject chaos. We want order. But too much order, too, can take a toll. Aggressive efforts to conquer chaos may defeat life and love as well.

Love, like safety, is not a given. It, too, requires effort. It is not inevitable. And though love may be what supports us in periods of chaos, some journeys in love upend our lives—the day the marriage shatters, the child dies, the forest disappears. Love, a comfort in chaos? The culprit, more likely! But here we accuse only some loves of breeding chaos. And even with love's risk of chaos, it is in our loves—and in Love itself—that we find support in the presence of chaos.

Crossing to safety when the world seems most dangerous, when we feel most alone and unloved, requires openness to viable love. This can be terribly difficult. The temptation is to indulge self-pity or to seek out counterfeit loves: laughter in a bottle, intimacy in a stranger, purposefulness in hectic activity. Some are fortunate enough to experience the unfailing love of God. Yet this path, we know, is not for everyone. Others find helpful love in the richness and wildness of the natural world. And some know how to consent to the supportive love to be found in the humanity of a friend or parent or sibling or community.

Winged Rock. Solid, yet in motion; seasoned by the past, accepting of the future. The mountain knows chaos. The mountain will not endure as mountain. And to the mountain, standing on its ledge, Paul and I returned the poem, where it remains today:

> Westward, wings of rock
> enfold the setting sun
> as the world tilts
> towards the edge of night.
>
> You have come this far
> and still you think
> your life will endure.

In time, the cycles of grief abated and I journeyed in the stage of acceptance. I surrendered in the battle to keep things the same. I relinquished the hope of bringing back the dead. All things die. Marriages, people, forests. Even mountains die.

"Till death do us part." There was a death, certainly. It parted us. The battle ended. The white flag rose, but not in defeat. There may be no resurrection, but there is rebirth.

❧

> Journal Entry: New Year's Day
>
> The bees came out today. A week ago I was afraid they were dead. It has been so cold. No sign of them—of life—for weeks. Then today the temperature soared into the 50s and the bees emerged—by the thousands. I fed them a little of their own honey.
>
> But this, this one thing I want to note: I had been so low. And then today when I saw my bees, my heart unbroken soared with them. The healing of insects. Who would have guessed?

❧

Every morning I reenact my climb up Shiprock. First I face the east and embrace Easter faith—hope and courage before the horizon. Next I turn south and conjure crops with deep roots in dark soil—steady growth and staying power in all kinds of weather. I face west and see the mountains—first the Shawangunks of the Hudson River Valley, then further west to Shiprock, which, in my mind, I climb again—with grace, dexterity, awareness, and skill—first with Paul, and then alone in Spirit. The west may hold danger, uncertainty, and hardship, but I climb still upwards. Finally, I face north and relinquish all imagery. In the darkness and silence and nakedness of the north I encounter something like rest, love, and communion. This is not the direction of hope, but rather the end of hope, its resolution.

Every morning, I return.

Part III

In Search of a University

Day Eight

The evening of day eight, we returned to Shiprock. As we approached the mountain for the second time that day, it appeared as a rip or tear in the sky, a ghostly opening into another world.

We drove to what some consider the front of the mountain, beneath which there is a small dirt parking lot. Paul set off in one direction to work on some poems, while I went directly upwards, notebook in hand. As I ascended, I became oblivious to everything except the uncertain rock I navigated. After about thirty minutes, I realized that, unlike earlier in the day when we climbed the backside of the mountain, I was now conspicuous to any onlookers. In the popular parking spot below me, several people stood or leaned against their cars. They were watching the sky and rock—and me. The Buddha warned, "A careless pilgrim only scatters the dust of his passions more widely."[40] I was now that careless pilgrim, an outsider, scattering dust and rock, drawing attention, distracting others from the purity of their worship—in this case, easygoing talk and relaxation among friends in the cool shade of the mountain. Some lessons are learned slowly. I moved as quickly as I could toward the west, where I hid myself behind a large boulder.

Not long afterward the mountain rewarded me greatly for my small act of penitence. I found my right side bathed suddenly in the rays of a bright golden sunset that, until then, had been concealed by Shiprock's stern. In that moment, the severe rock relented and both stone and man were illumined gently in the day's last light. Once again, something like healing took place high up on Winged Rock.

What I felt that evening on Shiprock is difficult to describe, for it was a single intricate moment in the flow of time—a complex convergence of sense and sensibility, of sight, sound, and touch, of longing, imagination, and love. John Dewey, the American pragmatist, had such poignant moments in mind when he wrote:

> There are moments of intense emotional appreciation when, through a happy conjunction of the state of the self and of the surrounding world, the beauty and harmony of existence is disclosed in experiences which are the immediate consummation of all for which we long.[41]

Yes—happy conjunction! Beauty and harmony disclosed! And in the moment itself, these experiences are often private, immediate, and profoundly simple. In her poem "Evening Star," Mary Oliver writes of what is easy and what is difficult for her to see:

> … certainly and easily I can see
> how God might be one rose bud,
> one white feather in the heron's enormous, slowly opening wing.
>
> It's after that
> it gets difficult.[42]

I am an educator. I teach in an institution of—as they say—higher education. In the academy, we focus on what is difficult to understand, and that is as it should be. Yet can we not, at least on occasion, speak of what is easy to see? Can I ask my students, "What is easy for you to see?" Can I tell them what is easy for me? What is it that is elevated in *higher* education that would keep us from reaching down to what is underlying and plain and fundamental? It is easy for Mary Oliver to "see how God might be one rose bud." It was easy for me to see, on my last visit to Shiprock, how God might be one sunset—how something as simple and everyday as a sunset could place my life in an expansive and curative perspective. Can I, as an educator, speak of this to my students? Can I, as an educator, neglect to? I want to speak on occasion of what is uncomplicated.

It's after that—after naming what comes easy in the way of sight or belief—that it gets difficult. In education we seldom rest or even pause in simplicity. Rushing into complexity is the norm. To explicate my encounter with that sunset behind Shiprock I would offer my students literary precedents. I might allude to what Wordsworth depicted as "a presence that disturbs my mind with the joy of elevated thought," and then I might place Wordsworth and the environmental imagination more generally in the historical context of Romanticism, thereby rendering my encounter with Shiprock as a Western, cultural production.

We academicians pose many questions. We gather evidence, offer justifications, and produce explanations, all the while making fine analytic distinctions and meticulous qualifications. This is what we do and do well. Still, I wonder: Is there a place in the classroom for what is easy? Is it ever appropriate to set aside our standard, methodical pursuit of critical knowledge? Can we occasionally embrace terminal simplicity and resist interminable complexity?

These are not abstract questions for me. They are practical. I confront them daily as an educator. Is a sunset or rosebud a legitimate academic subject? Can I take my students to a place to view the sunset or the rosebud? Can I speak of the beauty, fears, beliefs, and hopes that put me in motion—that underlie my actions, judgments, and feelings—without adding the customary qualification or discursive justification? Perhaps someday for me these worrisome questions will go away, dissipating like vapor on a bright day. Perhaps I will grow tired of such worries and just *teach*, just do what seems right regardless of the inward monitor that asks, "Can you really do this as a university professor?"

Recently I heard Emmet Gowin, the Princeton photographer, discuss his work. He had gotten over the question of legitimacy, if in fact he was ever preoccupied by it. He spoke of things of personal significance with ease and grace. He wasn't embarrassed to speak of what he loved or what he feared or what was plain for him to see. And because he was at ease, we—his audience of fifteen Vassar professors—were receptive to him. We granted ourselves license to hear him speak candidly of things known, like the pain of grief, and of things less known, like a face's revelation in a photograph. At one point he shed tears, and that, too, was acceptable. Vulnerability is perceptible in his photos; why not here in his presence? Gowin accepted himself, and we did likewise.

As he spoke, I awakened and thought, "Now, here's an educator." We the faculty had begun with our standard, formulaic academic questions ("Do you construct or deconstruct your subject matter?"), but we all quickly adjusted to our unusual guest. Repentant of our jargon and prescribed comments, reflective of our own lives, work, and world, we began to receive our guest and his work with openness and expectancy. Gowin transformed us, if only momentarily, into an intimate, sincere community of learning.

A community of learning—that's what educators want for their classrooms. If we are to build that community, perhaps our students require more than information, analytic skills, and such intellectual virtues as skepticism and "reductive" explanations. We may have to offer more of ourselves to ask more of our students. We may have to ask them on occasion, "What can you easily see? What do you know or believe?"

As I emerged from my crisis, I began to realize how hungry I had become to teach and write with heart. Since graduate school, I had maintained the rigorous, analytic practice that university education seemed to require of me, often choosing my subjects on the basis of their academic chicness rather than their ability to move and engage my students and me deeply and intuitively. It was time to make a change. The divide between the questions I addressed in the classroom and those I addressed in my everyday life had grown too great. As I worked to resuscitate my personal life, I began the process of resuscitating myself as a teacher—supplementing those safe academic questions with more trenchant, more consequential subjects. Relearning how to teach and write with heart became part of my search for a course.

At Princeton University, the graduate students live alone on a hill far away from campus, shops, and town. At the turn of the twentieth century, Woodrow Wilson, then president of Princeton, had fought against the off-campus location for the founding of the graduate school. Yet the vision of an elevated, cloistered graduate life prevailed. While Princeton has taken steps to integrate the graduate students into campus life, I spent my years there leading an almost monastic life of scholarship. As graduate students, we were disconnected not only from society but also from each other. I can hardly blame the university for such self-imposed isolation and the sadness that resulted, yet I cannot help but wish that Woodrow Wilson had gotten his way.

One night at around 3:00 a.m., my entire graduate dorm was awakened by a horrifying cry. "*Life, life, life!*" another student screamed repeatedly from his room. Curiously, we all seemed to understand his lament, and within a few minutes, most of us were milling about in the hallways, commiserating with the disturbed student, discussing our competitive academic pressures, our lack of community, our hollowness. A scream of agony had interrupted our sleep and brought us a moment of *communitas*. The next day, we were alone again, though one of us was missing.

❧

Good teachers often call themselves lifelong learners, and they encourage their students to think of themselves as lifers in this sense. But maybe there is some good in thinking of instructors and students alike as lifelong *educators*. For we are all teachers. We all know some things. And we impart some of what we know, daily.

College students read texts and write papers and show up for classes on Biopsychology or Urban Sociology or Victorian Poetry. These students know things about these subjects. Sometimes they know things about these subjects that no one else in the world knows. The classroom is a more vital place when all are asked and allowed to recognize and contribute what they know, to participate in a community of learning that stretches back to Confucius and Plato.

We are all teachers, then, and we are also all artists—struggling practitioners of the art of living. And there's more: we are all geniuses. That's right. This is not egalitarian flattery or a variety of the self-esteem movement. According to many classical traditions, genius has nothing to do with IQ scores or test-taking. All individuals *have* their genius—their particular voice, their perspective, their distinctive understanding of human flourishing—to offer to the community, to the common good, to the collective endeavor of our becoming human. In many Native American traditions, children are thought of as flickering fires, bright lights in need of shielding. The community works together to shelter and watch over these little lights, for each child has something the community will someday need.

My students are bright, yet their flames are often hidden. They sense little need to share them. For as long as they can remember, they have been surrounded by adult custodians: someone to cook their food, provide their clothes, drive them home, work the garden, paint the house, fix the plumbing, earn the money, and so on. What's more, they spend the great majority of their young lives in school, taught by instructors who have likely studied and taught for as many years as these students have lived. Teachers, too, are expert custodians.

What could these students offer to this world of custodians? They must wait and wait before they can contribute. As it turns out, nearly all schools are "prep schools" in the truest sense of the phrase, in that they are perpetually *preparing* our students for some life in the future. How far into the future? If these students decide to go to graduate school, they must wait on average twenty-nine years before their lives begin, before they are certified to contribute meaningfully to their communities.

That's a long wait. I want to ask my students *today*, "What can you certainly and easily see? What do you know or believe? What can you offer?" I want to begin now to see their gifts. More than that, I want them to see their gifts. Many teachers in physical education or shop departments identify a student's talent and enable her to develop it early on in her schooling. These students grow in skill and confidence by doing something practical and tangible. Like all humans, they take pleasure in doing something and doing it well.

I want my students, too, to craft something that is simple, practical, and elegant. I also of course want to engage them in what is complex and difficult, in the practices of qualification, distinction, and nuanced interpretation and explanation. After she tells us what is easy for her, Mary Oliver adds, "It's after that it gets difficult." She, too, is practiced in qualification. She knows she must attend vigilantly to the connection between her words and that which makes them true. Even poets have their meticulous standards—*especially* poets. Poets, like scientists, are obsessed with getting things right—with observing reality accurately, describing it truthfully, and testing their accounts rigorously. I am not speaking here epistemologically, as in a correspondence theory of truth, but aesthetically, morally, and spiritually, with respect to excellence and honesty. Frederick Sommer, an early mentor to Gowin, identified this common endeavor among scientists and poets:

> The world of art and the world of science
> are interested in evidence and verification.
>
> Art and science deal with evidence by way of position
> in a harmonious flow of linkages…
>
> [Art and science] are both interested in respect for reality
> and they are heavily weighed
> on the side of sense perception.[43]

It was early spring when I told Deirdre that I'd move out of the house and find an apartment. I didn't think of this as a generous gesture, though I was loath to move away from the chickens, the bees, the gardens, the woodlot, and the path that led through the woods to campus. I had lost my marriage, and I was now losing the land and creatures that had sustained me for the past year.

It was late afternoon. For weeks, I had wanted to talk about separating. Yet my mouth had refused to form that word—*separation.* I could see Deirdre in the kitchen making some herbal peach tea. I was in the living room adding wood to the stove, trying to kindle courage to utter the word that would bring about inexorable change. I knew that once it was spoken, that word that would formalize, publicize, and legalize the broken bond, that there would be no going back. How would she handle it? How would I? Would tears of sorrow or bitterness follow?

And then it happened. For a moment after I had said it, we stared at each other in silence, almost tenderly, feeling our lives shift into a new era. One word and the world had changed.

I offered to move out, but she replied, "No—I'll find a place. Probably in Ulster." As before, I learned that Deirdre had already considered our separation, had even made tentative logistical plans. I now suspect she had been patiently waiting for me to arrive at the conclusion that she had already grasped. Our conversation was remarkably short. We were courteous but unemotional. When she left the living room, her tea was still hot, the stove fully stoked, and our hearts coolly resigned.

There are at least two categories of "easy" and two of "difficult." Some things appear easy due to lazy, careless thinking. This kind of easy is not what I have in mind when I applaud Mary Oliver and Emmet Gowin for their willingness to state what they can certainly and simply see. Their ease does not come from indolent thinking or inattention to life's multiplicities. Nor does it come from discursive thought. It is, instead, the ease of perceiving what is inherently simple, plausible, and meaningful.

In some instances, this kind of easy could appear banal or corny. Are we willing to take that risk? Our students are sophisticated—almost as sophisticated as the professors they imitate. And, in my experience, sophisticates hate sentimentality more than they love wisdom. *Safer to say something that is trite yet critical than something that is thoughtful yet unsuspicious.* Education, though, has broader, more inclusive goals than sophistication. By allowing students to respond to what they can certainly and easily see, we might restore their intellectual naturalness, free them from paralyzing skepticism, and even dispel their self-consciousness about being wrong or sentimental. We might permit them to pursue wisdom without embarrassment.

As there are two kinds of easy, so there are two kinds of difficult. On the one hand, we can make things unnecessarily difficult. Tying ourselves into knots, we make "simple things complicated and complicated things impossible."[44] Much academic authorship falls under this category. We academicians bring to our questions an arsenal of fashionable jargon, abstract schemas, and specialized methodologies. I have spent much of my life deciphering difficult academic paragraphs, parsing and diagramming them to find often that their upshot was inconsequential or else significant but impossibly buried. We all know the story of the emperor who had no clothes. The contemporary academic paragraph suffers from the opposite condition: wearing so many layers as to obscure what's underneath.

But there exists the other kind of "difficult," the genuinely difficult, that is inherently rooted in reality. To meet genuine difficulty with too much tidiness or too little patience can lead to the error of simplification. In contrast, the nonsystematic, image-rich approach of the poet, for example, attempts to describe and explore truthfully some of life's innate difficulties. Here, honesty is the opposite of oversimplification.

Above, I complained about academic writing that obscures its subject matter. Anglo-American analytic writing, in contrast, prides itself on delivering ideas so clear, so distinct, that they make the prose of Descartes appear positively impressionistic. This admirable precision draws me consistently to contemporary analytic philosophy. Yet in placing so high a premium on clarity and distinction, the professional analytic philosopher increasingly eliminates uncertainty, ambiguity, and complexity; in doing, she neglects the presence of inherent messiness and vagueness. She narrows the scope of inquiry.

Some early American pragmatists, such as Charles Pierce and William James, understood that messiness and vagueness are often genuine features of our world and not only the results of deficient or sloppy knowledge. As philosophers, they were committed to the search for order, but not if that search denied the real presence of chaos. They were risk-takers. They were willing to investigate what I am calling the genuinely difficult.

The day after Deirdre and I decided to split up, I was back in the Vassar classroom at 2:00 p.m., teaching my course on religion and the environment. I had spent the previous night restless and wakeful and had risen in the dark around 4:00 a.m. to start my work. By the time my class began, the day already felt interminable. The assigned class reading was Leslie Silko's essay, "Landscape, History, and the Pueblo Imagination." I had taught it many times. I would generally begin class discussion around the second page, where Silko skillfully characterizes the Euro-American notion of landscape. This time, however, my approach was different. This time, I was struck by Silko's opening lines:

> You see that after a thing is dead, it dries up. It might take weeks or years, but eventually if you touch the thing, it crumbles under your fingers. It goes back to dust.[45]

Normally, I would have avoided such a seemingly tangential opening. But Silko's words haunted me: "You see that after a thing is dead, it dries up." Were these words, in fact, tangential? Could they address the heart of the essay? Could they address my own heart, the hearts of my students?

I took a deep breath, read aloud the opening sentences, and quietly asked: "What things in your life have died and dried up?" After a brief pause, the stories flowed—narratives laden with proper nouns: dead friends and pets, lands and relationships. Two students told of their parents' divorces. Instead of offering my own story, I steered the conversation toward the question, "Why does Silko begin with death and dust?"

With that question, my prepared lesson plan became irrelevant. Having reached deeply into their own lives by means of this prompt, the students now reached deeply into the essay at hand, making skillful discoveries and connections that were both familiar and novel to me. We discussed the role of dynamic, storied landscapes in the lives of the Pueblo and in our own lives. We spoke of how life and loss punctuate our lives and those of our communities, and how we ultimately return to and rest in the land from which we drew life; we noted that to understand as much, the cycle of dust to dust, is to understand where our home is—that all of us, one way or another, live among corn and rinds and bones—and to these we must return. Together, we learned much about birth, death, and rebirth in the Pueblo tradition, and what it might mean for our lives.

Our discoveries were not especially systematic or analytic, but they were truthful, instructive, and genuinely complex.

I admire the art and beauty of analytic philosophy. I love the craft of making fine distinctions, formulating clear statements, and doing honest conceptual work. The love of this work propelled me through graduate school, drove me to teach, and sustained me when I lacked other sources of life and love.

I do seek additional tools, however. I want more pedagogical options than the ones rationalistic analyses provide. Gowin's photography is rigorous, detailed, and, in its way, deeply traditional. It seems to me to embody the classical academic virtues. But Gowin, too, seeks something more, something as novel as ancient. So he took to the mountaintop—an ancient place—and from there he discovered new vistas.

I am referring to Gowin's aerial photography: landscapes photographed from airplanes. He chose to soar ten thousand feet and rediscover thus a familiar world from new heights. Granting distance to his subject matter, Gowin permits landscapes to manifest their autonomy. There is something loving in this work. It is the opposite of manipulation, though it remains artful in its craft. To grant or to recognize the agency of the natural world is to facilitate something like revelation. Gowin's lens *subjects us* to the land's capacity to *expose us* to something new. In the process, we become the land's subject.

This is what I want for my work and for my classroom: the emergence of the marvelous between the familiar and the unfamiliar. I want academics as we know it but also academics as it was known long ago, when philosophers thought that walking and teaching might belong together, that friendship and beauty were topics of serious consideration, and that contemplation was one of the great sources of human joy and understanding. I want to expose my students—as Gowin exposes us—to horizons beyond those of the contemporary, specialized classroom, which, despite its emphasis on modernity, postmodernity, and globalization, is in many ways deeply parochial. Again, I do not mean this as an indictment of the academy. It works, and in most ways works well. But it does constrain. It is fearful of what it considers unconventional—which today may include that which is deeply traditional.

Paul and I are respectable scholars. We publish in reputable peer-reviewed journals. We participate at professional conferences and teach solid, credible courses. We have, as they say, reputations to maintain. Yet suddenly we had, almost by accident, created a course dealing with contemplation, a course whimsically entitled, *It's Only Natural: Contemplation in the American Landscape*. What is more, we had studied with two Native American teachers for whom contemplation—or something like it—is as natural as eating or reading. In most institutions today, studying contemplation is questionable and engaging in contemplative exercises downright scandalous. Would Paul and I then study and discuss contemplative traditions and their relation to the land without actually engaging our students in contemplative practices? Would we investigate the concept without incorporating the activity?

In many ways, the contemporary university classroom is a place open to broad-minded intellectual pursuits and exploration. The standards by which educational material is deemed acceptable or unacceptable are necessary and constructive. Any educative setting—whether a cooking lesson at home, a political lesson in the streets, or a moral lesson in the beauty salon—is informed, regulated, and sustained by the relevant customs. These dictate, among other things, what count as worthy questions and goals, approaches and techniques, standards of excellence and measures of advancement. These customs, if treated respectfully as both necessary and provisional, typically change over time and are subject to thoughtful revision. They can also, however, become ossified and resistant to change.

During the twentieth century and especially after World War II, American colleges and universities increasingly promoted what we consider rigorous, specialized scientific education. This is not to say that the arts and letters are not also supported. But scientific curricula—in all their plurality—have become the central paradigm for legitimate university education. By and large, those working in the arts and letters—that is, in "soft" subjects usually located in humanities departments—either attempt to imitate the sciences or settle for slightly lower status in the university.

Settling for lower status—or learning to ignore such status—can often benefit and liberate a professor. But imitating scientific approaches can do much harm to the vocation of the teacher-scholar. I am not, of course, opposed to the sciences. What could such opposition possibly mean? I began as a math and physics major in college and have never regretted that training. I have attempted to cultivate a variety of virtues embedded in the practices of scientific research—patience, attentiveness, conscientiousness, imaginative openness, and humility among them. I harbor a healthy respect for the empirical, for a tangible world that operates by its own laws, independent of my personal wants and desires; a world to study and engage and listen to. Moreover, the natural sciences have taught me, by example, that there should be a place in the university to study such everyday, practical issues as breast cancer and climate change.

My complaint, then, is not about the sciences or the high regard that skillful scientific research and teaching receive. My complaint is about the humanities' poor imitation of the sciences and, to that end, the anxious rejection of approaches and subjects that do not fit within their increasingly narrow paradigms. A mandate of the university is to study the universe. No aspect of the universe, then, should be judged, in advance, to be outside the bounds of inquiry, and no thoughtful approach should be rejected simply because it does not yield the kinds of results (usually quantifiable and replicable) generated by "hard" sciences. Yet the prejudice in favor of science is in place, and it informs such practical issues as what research is funded and which courses are taught. I desire a university culture that does not make it difficult to reach beyond the academy's standard methods and approaches for other, additional tools.

The math of marital separation is easy enough: you only need to know how to perform a division by two, what mathematicians call a *mediation.* Property divides easily; lives split with more difficulty. And what of beauty? Is it, too, subject to division? "It is essential to prove that beauty may be in small, dry things."[46] When T. E. Hulme wrote that line, he was trying to show that beauty should not be confined to the grandiose, the infinite, or "the beyond." Rather, beauty lives in the everyday patterns of our lives. Silko and Hulme, then, would both caution us against consigning beauty to the sublime landscape or celestial love. Beauty is found among corn and rinds and bones.

As Deirdre searched for a new residence and began packing her things, and as I added books to newly emptied shelves and read online forums about separation and divorce, beauty did appear in "small, dry things." Our last days together were unquestionably mundane and resigned, and yet we would on occasion find ourselves gazing at each other with gentleness and consideration, even affection. The marriage had dried up and crumbled. The scent of death still lingered. Yet so did beauty, however muted.

Aristotle maintained that the highest forms of human knowledge and happiness stem from contemplation. But so did the religious thinker, Thomas Aquinas, and hence the problem: contemplation could be considered a *religious* practice. Never mind that in the ancient Mediterranean world, philosophy was often regarded as a practice—a way of life—that greatly resembled what we today call religion, that is, comprehensive beliefs and practices that pertain to deep questions of human suffering, identity, purpose, and happiness. In today's university—and in departments of religious studies in particular—activity that approximates religious activity is usually barred. This, I suspect, is why "practical" activities are also deemed questionable. Religion and the practice of ancient philosophy often address the cultivation of the whole person, including her relation to the greater society. Moral, aesthetic, economic, and physical aspects of life were all included in what we could call the ancient philosophical or traditional view of education. Yet this approach often conflicts with that of the contemporary research university.

The traditional approach is decidedly *material.* If we practiced such pedagogy today, moral inquiry would explore not only abstract questions about ethics or rights, but also practical issues pertaining to our students' relation to local public schools, prisons, and community service organizations. An aesthetic schooling would include classes not only in art history but also in the work of local artisans and in students' own artistic skills. Economics courses would develop not only theoretical economic models but also strategies to enhance the university's involvement with local businesses and farms, studying local outcomes of national and global policies. And the physical would refer not only to string or M-theory but also to such material activities as dance and meditation, on the one hand, and recycling, sustainable building construction, and renewable energy, on the other. This is what I am calling a *material* education in contrast to the contemporary university's *abstract* approach, which treats the student as a disembodied mind with little or no connection to a place, a set of passions, and a body. For all its fear of spirituality, the university is among the most spiritualized places on earth.

I want to be careful here. I don't want to be unfair. Hyperbole will not advance the cause of understanding or reform. As I enumerate my complaints I am reminded of my diligent colleagues who are open to almost any approach and material as long as good work is being done. Thinking of them makes me believe I exaggerate here. But I am reminded also of other colleagues, equally diligent and conscientious, reading these pages with their eyes rolling. What are their concerns? What do they fear? Why, for example, would they object to my leading students in a contemplative exercise during the first or last five minutes of class every other week or so? Perhaps they fear that my course somehow gives all courses a bad name or that it is simply inappropriate.

If I sound a bit defensive in these pages, it is in part because I myself am not entirely comfortable with all this talk of contemplation and broadening pedagogical approaches. I'm still more at ease with the manners and methods of what we now call the traditional classroom: analyzing primary texts with the help of secondary material; formulating issues that are easily converted into exam questions or paper topics; evaluating students on their accumulation of knowledge and their ability to make a compelling argument to the satisfaction of the profession. This is how I was schooled; this is how I typically teach. It has many merits. It is what our students now expect. But, as I have said, I want more.

Am I ready for more? Probably not. After all, think what might happen if I were to engage students on a deeper level. (No, not on a deeper level, but on *more* levels.) Some students would not like the course. It would depart too radically from what they are accustomed to. Others, however, might become animated—experience alertness—as they wake up in the classroom. These students might want to have additional meetings outside regular classroom hours. They might bring to class salient readings or art to enhance the classroom discussion. This, in turn, could lead to a departure from the syllabus and could even lead to conversations in which I, the professor, am no longer the sole expert. Students might report to me about how the course connects to, and causes them to reflect on, other parts of their lives. These students might come to expect much from me—expect me to respond to their animation, their deeply felt questions, their desire to pursue a wide range of topics flowing beyond the course material. The students might recruit other students and disclose to their parents, teachers, and administrators what is happening in this class that is no longer just a class. Much could happen. Much that terrifies me—and most of my university colleagues.

Annie Dillard, I believe, is the kind of traditionalist I want to champion. Listen, for example, to her classical account of why we read:

> Why are we reading, if not in hope of beauty laid bare, life heightened and its deepest mystery probed?...Why are we reading if not in hope that the writer will magnify and dramatize our days, will illuminate and inspire us with wisdom, courage, and the possibility of meaningfulness, and will press upon our minds the deepest mysteries, so we may feel again their majesty and power?...We should amass half dressed in long lines like tribesmen and shake gourds at each other, to wake up....[47]

I want to talk to my students of the "hope of beauty laid bare." I want them to encounter "life heightened and its deepest mystery probed." I want them to connect their education with such virtues as wisdom and courage. I want us to shake gourds at each other and wake ourselves up.

Each morning after reading Thomas Merton's *New Seeds of Contemplation,* I study my bookmark. It's a crinkled photograph of Paul and me, shingling the roof of a towering red barn. Talk about higher education! This picture is my morning koan, my chance for spiritual awakening. Yet I never know what to make of it. It seems to speak to me about a higher purpose of work, but it also causes me to recollect the immense fear I felt up there. That barn is high—as tall as a six-story building. Paul and his friends walked so gracefully, fearlessly, on the steep-pitched roof. I, in contrast, went straight to the roof ridge and held on for dear life, doing a little work with a scraper. And yet, each day I return to the barn, hoping it will reveal something to me—something beyond my fear.

I wonder how many students in higher education feel like me up on that roof, holding on with all their might, longing to make the elevated moves that others around them seem to make? Could the fear itself—the risk—be central to education, to the task of growth? In my fear I was fully awake. What must we risk for education?

Is contemplation in the classroom acceptable? Paul, our students, and I made progress in the ways of contemplation, and we found the results quite practical. As the teachers, Paul and I had to learn to become comfortable leading the students in contemplative exercises. This task required that we gain a deeper and broader understanding of contemplative techniques. Mostly, however, we needed to undergo a shift in attitude. As I have been saying all along, it isn't easy—intellectually or emotionally—to depart from standard classroom procedures. Paul and I needed to believe that this and other departures from the classroom status quo were valid. We used to ask ourselves, only half joking, "Is this course legitimate? Can we really get away with this?" We would smile and shake our heads as if to say, "No—we are frauds as educators." Yet both of us, I think, also harbored the unspoken belief that this was the most legitimate course we had ever taught—that in this course, perhaps for the first time, we had allowed ourselves to endeavor to build a community of learning, a place of trust for intellectual, moral, and emotional growth and engagement.

The students, in contrast to their professors, were not at all self-conscious. From the start they were mostly ready to embrace this new pedagogical adventure. Moreover, they seemed hungry for a course that treated them as whole adults and not unformed, disembodied minds.

I remember well the first day of class. The syllabus announced the first topic of the course: "*Inner & Outer Landscapes* Introduction: A Dance of Concepts." And that's just what we did—we danced.

After we reviewed the syllabus, a live band played music and a caller led us in a series of lively contra dances, many of which were inspired by local places and events. The fiddle, guitar, banjo, accordion, and flute were the grammar of our first lesson. The caller was the principal educator, instructing us in the art of each dance, leading us in the "walkthrough" in which we would imitate the patterned steps. And the students (including Paul and me) were the community of learners as well as the topic for the day. With no gendered roles and no lasting partner, we all led, we all followed. On that first day we caught a glimpse of the fluid, embodied connection—the dynamic dance—between individual and group, mind and body, and inner and outer landscapes. On that day we understood that this course would not be like other courses. It would lead us to places of delight, wonder, and integrated learning. And I can tell you in advance that, in practical ways, the contemplative exercises helped us reach those places.

Did contemplation bring us enlightenment or an experience of the sublime? Such were never our goals. No more mysterious than most educational objectives, our aims were decidedly material and practical. As individuals and as a group, we achieved moments of stillness, alertness, and focus. We became skillful in being attentive to a particular feature of a text, of the land, and of the relation between the two; in letting go of distracting worries rooted in the past or looming in the future; in being open to fresh and various ways of understanding a subject; in inviting, but not insisting on, a beneficial calm. Such skills, especially in the context of an increasingly fast-paced society, are what I refer to as the course's *practical* objectives.

❧

I have gained much respect for the practical during my search for a course. As we visit the territories of vulnerability, injury, and healing, we often acquire a heightened sense of our fellow travelers in these regions, which, in turn, comes with an enhanced desire to offer practical assistance, insofar as we can, to those who have lost their sense of direction. Sometimes, simply offering our own stories of loss and healing can be greatly helpful.

My students have lives. Like the rest of us, they struggle to gain footing as they experience vulnerability and injury. When I, as an educator, know and *see* my students, I want on occasion to offer them something tangible and practical, something to help them name their location and find their heading. This basic form of care is a deeply traditional facet of education. Tlingit Indian elders, for example, have long brought practical care to their educational tasks.

Prior to graduate school, I lived for some time in Angoon, Alaska—the only settlement on Admiralty Island, a town of about five hundred Tlingits. There was much to love about Angoon: the natural beauty, the openhearted people, the uncluttered existence in which one could encounter the fundamentals of life—birth and death, food and shelter, society and solitude. Angoon's location is stunningly beautiful, but dangerous, too: turn in one direction, toward the sea, and you are confronted with the treacherous tidal channel, Chatham Strait, or *Shee ya* as the Tlingits call it; turn the other way, you are met by a dense, enticing temperate rainforest. Between the two is the thin strip of safe dwelling, Angoon.

I once explored a little way into the forest. I had spent much time in my youth hiking in the Bay Area coastal mountains and in the high Sierras, and I was confident in my sense of direction. On this occasion, however, I soon became lost. In this rainforest, there was no sun, hills, apparent topography, or horizon to provide a sense of direction. Everywhere I surveyed, there were ferns, lichens, and tall, dense trees. Thick moss coated every surface. I remained calm for the first hour or so and then I panicked. The temperature began to drop and I began to scramble. In my haste, I tripped on a downed branch and gashed my knee. I was about to stand and resume my flight, when a line of poetry, astonishingly, held me in place. It was the title and first line of a Tlingit-Haida poem that my Tlingit "uncle," William Nelson (or *Tah-in*), had recited to me two years earlier:

> What Do I Do When I Am Lost in the Forest?
> *Stand still.*

And that's what I did. I took some deep breaths, nursed my knee, and repeated over and over and again, "What do I do when I am lost in the Forest? *Stand still.*" Later in life a poet would save my life, but back then it was a poem.

Like most of us, students must rush through their days. They, too, have little time or opportunity to pay attention to their emotional, bodily, or intellectual state, much less to those around them. Like us, they are deeply grateful for opportunities to pause, to turn off the screen, to look around and within, to awaken to the present. In the contemplative exercises that Paul and I led—however short and infrequent—we as a class became increasingly confident in a process, in a way of learning, in a type of embodied thinking and human growth. We were reminded, to paraphrase Emily Dickinson, how startling a thing it is to live.

Toward the end of the course we took a field trip to Mohonk Mountain in the Hudson River Valley. Twenty students and two professors walked in complete silence for half an hour from the Mohonk parking lot, through the Mountain House, and up a windy path into the dramatic Shawangunk Mountains. After this initial walking meditation we gathered in silence, looking below at the emerald lake that borders the majestic

Mountain House and, further below, the great sunken sweep of the Mohonk Valley. I spoke briefly about the geological history of the place, and, after a protracted silence, Paul discussed its cultural and literary history. More silence. Eventually, some students posed questions and comments before we embarked on another silent walk, this time to the Sky Tower. From that high, stony edifice we had a panoramic view of the entire range of the Northern Shawangunks, running north-south and flanked by the Mohonk Valley to the west and the Hudson River Valley to the east. If the earlier silence had been due in part to the discipline of walking meditation, the silence now was more a natural, unaffected response to this place at this moment—a place whose art and literature we had studied intermittently over the previous four months. In the silence, our learning was made more complete.

Up on that tower it occurred to me that perhaps Paul or I should offer some guidance, some commentary. Paul, as if hearing my thoughts, said quietly, "They know what to do now."

Yes, they knew what to do. The students—and their professors—had acquired a skill. They had gained some proficiency in the art of seeing—though "listening" is as appropriate a metaphor, if a metaphor it is. As they walked through the land known as Mohonk, they saw much. They had come prepared with useful knowledge about Mohonk, its cultural and natural history, the songs and literature it had inspired, the streams and animals it harbored. But they had brought, too, the capacity to journey in a place with quietude and attentiveness—with openness, broad perspective, and affection.

This capacity to know how to approach a place—to ask of it questions from different perspectives, to allow it to pose questions in return, and to allow silence—is a practical skill. It could also be called a mode of contemplation. Like reading or writing, it could easily become a frequent practice in our lives. Skill in contemplation and the concomitant capacity to pay attention to what is before us can greatly assist our daily lives: encountering an unfamiliar situation or text, talking to a friend, walking down the street, preparing a meal, being lost in a forest. It can mean the difference between conscientious engagement and habitual apathy, thoughtful responses and reactive behavior, sensitivity to someone's hour of greatest need and the failure even to notice it. Yet because this is a practical, "life" skill, as opposed to a narrowly defined academic one, the cultivation of this approach is largely absent from the university's educational mission.

How long are we to remain in silence? How long before we begin naming again? Silly questions. There is a delicate dance, a constant interplay, between naming and silence, each taking the lead when appropriate. Life and learning without silence are text on a page without spaces: crowded, chaotic, difficult to parse. A more serious question, then: Can the university honor the place and role of silence?

Tlingits teach their children to respect the forest in different ways. One way is to frighten them with stories about *Kushdaka*, a large land otter that hypnotizes those who wander without knowledge into the forest. As *Kushdaka* projects familiar signs to them, the victims are led deep into the dark woods. Once far from the safety of home, the victims are irreversibly transmogrified into *Kushdaka*.

Another way to educate children about the forest is by means of the poem that *Tah-in* had taught me. It is a practical poem. It is meant to save lives.

> What Do I Do When I Am Lost in the Forest?
>
> Stand still.
> The trees ahead and bushes beside you are not lost.
> Wherever you are is called "Here,"
> And you must treat it as a powerful stranger,
> Must ask permission to know it and be known.

Listen, the forest breathes.
It whispers, "I have made this place around you."
If you leave it, you may come back again saying, "Here."

No two trees are the same to raven,
No two branches are the same to wren.
If what a tree or branch does is lost on you,
Then you are surely lost.

Stand still,
The forest knows where you are.
You must let it find you.[48]

As I sat on the ground, lost in the forest, clutching my hurt knee, repeating the opening lines of the poem, panic gradually turned to gentle stillness. The poem, not *Kushdaka*, reached me first. I was not lost. I was visiting a place called "here." In standing still, I was found.

In my newly found calm, I surveyed my situation. "No two trees are the same to raven, no two branches are the same to wren." The trees and branches *were* different—in age, shape, size, and, looking up, in brightness. In one direction, the highest branches tended to be a bit more illuminated. I stood up, faced the direction of the brighter, tall branches, and assumed that the sun was at my back. It was evening time—which in late May continues for hours—so I figured I was facing east, opposite the setting sun. Angoon is on the tip of a peninsula that runs north-south, so if I could stay on course to the east or west, I would reach the shoreline and I could then travel north along it to the village. Two hours later I reached the Angoon Native Brotherhood Hall. This, then, is how a practical poem saved me.

I remembered when I first offered my students the poem. I was teaching a course called *Love: the Concept and Practice*. In the first weeks of the semester, we read Louise Erdrich's *Love Medicine* along with Plato's *Symposium*. Both books, I suggested, are about what it is to be lost and found, and about how beauty and love, if invited into our lives, can lead us home even if the path is difficult and the homecoming imperfect. And so I started a class session with the poem, introducing it with my own story of losing and finding my bearings in Alaska. I read the poem because it illuminated my account of Erdrich and Plato. But that's not the only reason. I was glad for this occasion to offer my students this practical gift. I told them there would be time in their lives—in the challenge of a class project, a broken relationship, an illness, a hope dashed, a fear realized—when this poem could help them find their way. The class ended in liturgical response. Three times I asked, "What do I do when I am lost in the forest?" and three times the students replied in unison, "Stand still."

Contemplation is only too practical for a university culture that derives its identity from its position outside the everyday needs and language of the surrounding communities. These, however, are the very communities from which students come and to which they will soon return. Nonetheless, cultivating "mind skills," and not "life skills," has become the role of the university. The standard defense, then, relies on a pedagogical division of labor: in the university students learn academic skills; outside the university they learn everything else.

One evident problem is that this division of labor imposes an artificial—and ultimately unworkable—separation of academic skills from the very material or content these skills are meant to address. What are students to read *about*? What are students to write *about*? What are students to apply statistical models *to*? The university's implicit answer is that students are to study what is most distant—dead authors, faraway lands, global economies. Local economies, regional cultural and natural histories, and practical skills: these are too close to home to qualify as matters of serious academic pursuit. The university's tendency to discount the practical and the local results from their classification as ordinary and parochial and therefore unworthy of *higher* education. For the same reason, when a professor thinks and writes about teaching and learning, it is not considered significant academic work. It is too experiential, too relevant to daily, local practice.

If educators do bring into the classroom "the things of ordinary experience,"[49] a natural connection between locality and practicality often emerges. By directing students' attention to some local phenomena, we inevitably bring about confrontation with practical issues. We start by asking little questions, like how to arrive somewhere, and soon we are asking larger questions, like how did this six-lane road get placed here, bisecting this impoverished neighborhood? We explore the Poet's Walk by the Hudson and contemplate the river, and soon we start to wonder, how far to the north run the headwaters of the Hudson? How far to the south is the Indian Point nuclear power plant? Where is the intake for our drinking water, and just how deeply buried in the bed of the river are those General Electric PCBs? The Hudson may begin at Lake Tear of the Clouds in the Adirondacks, but at some point it flows both ways.

Terry Tempest Williams once wrote, "It may just be that the most radical act we can commit is to stay home."[50] She is challenging us to know and care for a place. She is recommending local knowledge. How are we to talk of things global with no understanding of things close to home? But where is our home? What is our home? These questions, for obvious reasons, have become important to me, and I now find myself asking them of my students. Turns out, home is a pressing issue for them, too.

Students offer various depictions of home, some familiar, some less so. Home is the place of their parents or the campus and the community around it; home is located in their social media activity or in their relationships with friends; home is something they carry within themselves, a moveable sanctuary. When I ask them for their stories about home, I often hear accounts of being lost and then found. Students are on a journey, too. They are searching for a place of belonging.

Paul and I wanted our coursework to flow both ways, toward inner and outer growth. We wanted to teach out of particulars. By that I mean that we wanted to utilize the particularity of the local history and landscapes of the Hudson River Valley as well as the particularity of each member in the course—another, different kind of local knowledge. This route to knowledge incorporates two different, yet related, paths: the local and the inward. Socrates exemplifies the inward path in his attempt to follow the counsel of the oracle at Delphi, "Know yourself." This quest for knowledge can take place anywhere if the self is sufficiently mindful. Emerson exemplifies the local path. He advises, "The soul is no traveler; the wise man stays at home." Local learning allows us to acknowledge the vast and complex paths that lie immediately outside our front doors if only we have eyes to see them.

Again, I do not deny that travel can be useful in this journey. Think of Navajo Ben Barney traveling to Germany. Also, I do not advocate insularity, or ignorance of our connections to global networks—cultural, political, and economic—or dismissal of how these networks affect communities near and far. My worry lies with the practice of passing over and disregarding the local en route to the foreign and global. As long as we fixate on things faraway, we shun the burden of studying the form and condition of our own lives and communities. And when we shun self-knowledge and community-knowledge, we discount the obligations and benefits that emerge in the relation between self and community. Gratitude and social justice start close to home. Self-knowledge, and the education that encourages it, is as practical as it is urgent, for it pertains to, as Socrates once put it, "how we ought to live our lives."[51]

If we are to tackle such problems as discrimination, economic injustice, or environmental degradation—problems that have both a personal and an institutional face—then we need to provide students not only with specialized information and critical arguments, but also with nurtured, practical concerns for such democratic values as honoring human dignity and committing to shared projects. Cultivating such dispositions requires nourishing both the student's interior life and her community life. These dispositions cannot be achieved alone, in private. Again, we arrive at a classical understanding of pedagogy: the education of the whole person for the sake of personal and societal flourishing.

Aristotle's *Nicomachean Ethics*, which he wrote for his students, states that the goal of inquiry is "not in order to know what virtue is, but in order to become good."[52] Academic knowledge (in the narrow sense) is secondary to the goal of practical skill—skill in goodness. This is not anti-intellectualism on the part of Aristotle. Careful, critical, analytic moral inquiry marks his approach and style (sometimes to the dismay of undergraduates who find his precision and nuance daunting). The point is that the aim of Aristotle's careful, analytic work is practical: "to become good." Can this practical aim be part of the mission of the university?

The practical, as I am using the term here, should not be construed as the utilitarian, if by utilitarian we mean the pursuit of narrow, no-nonsense, "pragmatic" (think, "hardheaded") goals that do not include such pursuits as beauty or justice or a sense of belonging. That which is the least utilitarian can turn out to be the most practical. We hear people referring to reading, writing, and arithmetic as components of a utilitarian education because these components, it is held, will someday get us jobs. Around the season of university and school budget cuts, the argument is often made that the arts and physical education, for example, are not utilitarian and may even be considered frivolous.

But what if beauty in art or teamwork in soccer can save a life? They can, you know. Art and athletics can contribute in a variety of ways to human flourishing. They contribute to a balanced, joyful life. This is practical. Joy is practical. What could be more practical than joy?

I have a friend named Brent. We have known each other since the start of our lives. Our mothers, who were as close as sisters, were pregnant with us at the same time. The frequency of my contact with Brent has waxed and waned over the decades, but our friendship is solid, based more on a shared history than on a shared vision. When his twelve-year-old son struggled with and then died of cancer, our connection and history greatly deepened.

During my separation with Deirdre, Brent and I went backpacking in the John Muir and Ansel Adams wilderness areas of the high Sierras for ten days. On the seventh day of hiking above 10,000 feet among John Muir's favorite mountains and valleys, we set up camp for the evening and I left to find water. It had been a dry summer and so my search led me far from camp. By the time I found a small pool, darkness had come. I was confident that I knew the way back. But soon enough, I began to have my doubts, heading one way, then another. In the dark, I could not find the sites that I had noted to lead me back to home base. And once again, the voices of panic sounded: You have no food, you have no bedding, you could freeze.

Trying to suppress these voices, I pushed on. Indeed, I moved faster, branches now occasionally whipping my face and body, but I knew that I would indeed remain lost if I could not conquer the panic. I needed to use what I had learned from my past experiences of being lost. Like the Tlingit poem said, I needed to stand still.

I stopped. I waited. I listened. In that silence, I gathered myself, found myself, and then I heard it: an indistinct sound like a foghorn in the night. I traveled toward it. I was now avoiding the branches, walking more deliberately. I had a destination. The repetitive sound became louder. After about fifteen minutes of this, I discerned a faint glow in the direction of the sound. Eventually, the sound became clearer, as did the sight: there was my friend, Brent, up on an elevated rock, holding a lit lantern high in the air, shouting, "Mark…Mark…Mark."

Again, I was saved by a voice and a light not my own. As Brent's voice and light led me out of the cold and darkness to the warmth and safety of our camp, I couldn't help but think of my recent darkness in Poughkeepsie and of the light and hope that friendship can bring. Homecoming arrives in various ways. Years ago I would not have talked to my students about "home," much less understood their claim that home can be that place of care between friends. Understanding as much is another form of local, practical knowledge.

In *Hard Times*, Charles Dickens vividly imagines a purely utilitarian education. The students first arrive at "M'Choakumchild school" with bright imaginations and a hunger to learn, but the school's narrow curriculum and harsh teaching style soon starve the students spiritually and even disfigure some of them. Mr. Thomas Gradgrind, the owner of the school, is "a man of realities," we are told, "a man of facts and calculations…. With a rule and a pair of scales, and the multiplication table always in his pocket, ready to weigh and measure any parcel of human nature, and tell you exactly what it comes to."[53] There is no room for moral creativity or quieting (or disquieting) beauty in Gradgrind's classroom.

I have suggested that university culture is nervous about and suspicious of the practical. But what of the utilitarian? In the past, liberal arts colleges and universities have been able to resist those utilitarian, social pressures that would turn their undergraduate curriculums into explicit training for the professions. There are, however, two recent developments that threaten to reduce a robust liberal arts education in favor of preparing students for the job market.

The first pertains to the students themselves. More than ever, students see a liberal arts education as a ticket to a job or to a graduate degree that will bring future success in their professions in law, business, and medicine, for example. Of course, a well-rounded liberal arts education *does* provide excellent training for the professions. Future success in a profession, however, should be seen as a secondary or indirect consequence of excellence in education. When it becomes the chief aim of education, universities and their professors become mere apparatuses in the preparation of workers for the marketplace. There is much social pressure on students—and increasingly on universities—to see education as the cultivation of marketable credentials and skills. Here, education only accommodates the pre-established demands of the job market.

The second development threatening liberal arts education is the direct relationship that universities are cultivating with market industries. More and more, universities are forming partnerships with private companies, who have the funds and the demand for researchers with new ideas, designs, and techniques. The university, in turn, supplies researchers in need of funding. As a result of this partnership, university research projects are increasingly directed by market forces.

The university's laboratories and courses are currently driven by two horses: one pulling toward the liberal arts as a celebration of the breadth and depth of knowledge for its own sake, and one pulling toward the application and profit of education within the marketplace. The horses, in my view, are not good and evil, but representative of different sets of legitimate goals.

Theory alone (knowledge for its own sake) may become self-indulgent, leading students to gaze detachedly from the

Ivory Tower, largely disregarding practical, daily issues. Conversely, practice alone may become excessively utilitarian, leading students to view a liberal arts education primarily as a means to a successful career, and leading the university's business relationships with private industry to dictate its teaching and research aims.

For the sake of clarity, allow me to say again: Students should be encouraged to bring to their studies such practical concerns as "How does this material benefit my community, my society, my world, and my pursuit of maturation?" Moreover, it would be naïve and elitist to disparage the student who sees a connection between education and future vocational aims. The danger lies in the prospect of education becoming nothing but a means to a vocational end (whose value is explicitly tied to the figures of a post-graduate salary). Similarly, universities should be encouraged to bring their expertise and resources to the world outside their gates. It is appropriate for the university to seek collaborative projects with industries in order to develop and disseminate new technologies, procedures, and knowledge. But the university must maintain its own educational mission and not slavishly chain itself to the market's bearing.

There are two horses, then, with their own proper goals, desires, and drives—*theoria* and *praxis*—and the university struggles to honor and to steer both with some accord.

England had been mostly industrialized by 1854, the year Charles Dickens depicted the "melancholy madness" of Coketown in *Hard Times.* The workers' apathy, factories' environmental pollution, and the growing wage gap in fictional Coketown conjure many real American towns whose populations migrated with the steam engine from the agricultural fields to urban industrial centers. With factories came specialized labor, and with specialized labor came the proliferation of commodities and complex systems of exchange, and from these came much wealth, great inequality, and the beginning of universal, compulsory education. These developments begged new questions of established traditions about how and why to educate.

"What is the relation between education and industry?" is still a chief question among educators today. Is education's primary purpose to cultivate character and broad, critical engagement with the world, or is it to provide specialized and scientific training to serve industrial careers? Thomas Huxley, at the opening of Mason Science College in Birmingham, England in 1880, famously argued for the importance of a technical, scientific education; Matthew Arnold, responding to Huxley in his essay, "Literature and Science," defended a liberal arts education that consisted mostly of classical literature in Greek and Latin.

It is customary to portray these standpoints as diametrically opposed: in one corner, Huxley, champion of a new scientific education fitting the industrial age; in the other corner, Arnold, defender of a traditional liberal arts education for the ennoblement of student character. Vocationally driven, utilitarian training shuns tradition while impractical literary education eschews innovation—these are the arguments handed down to us from critics of each camp.

The disagreement between Huxley and Arnold, however, was not nearly so polarized. Huxley was never interested in reducing education to purely utilitarian (and certainly not to purely vocational) ends. He explicitly opposed a reductive approach to education, maintaining that the practical implications of theory often could not be immediately grasped.[54] Arnold, for his part, disregarded neither innovation nor practicality. Practical benefits, he argued, flow from a traditional, liberal arts education. "The best which has been thought and said in the world"—that is, the classics—is a tremendous resource for society that offers perhaps "great help out of our present difficulties."[55]

Huxley and Arnold, then, were not as opposed as it may seem. Yet the hyperbolized debate has taken on its own life, and to this day we are asked to participate in it, asked to choose between the humanities and the sciences, between theory and practice, or between tradition and innovation. The mark of a fine liberal arts education, however, is a dynamic, interdisciplinary approach to a wide variety of questions and issues that cross the very boundaries exaggerated in caricatures of the Huxley-Arnold debate.

In class I recently read from the concluding chapter of Kant's *Critique of Practical Reason*:

> Two things fill the heart with ever new and increasing awe and reverence, the more often and the more steadily we meditate upon them: the starry firmament above and the moral law within.

An earnest and sincere student asked, "I get the reference to the stars, meaning our connection to the external world of the senses; but what on earth is this internal world, this law within?" Yes, what on earth is this internal world that can fill the heart with awe and reverence? It is "on earth." It can be studied. Yet the university today is far better at approaching the stars above than those within.

What, then, did divide Huxley and Arnold? The stars above versus the stars within? Each man feared what education would become if it followed the trajectory implicit in the logic of his challenger. Arnold feared that Huxley's scientific education could lead to a system wherein literature would be dethroned and science would become a purely applied discipline, dedicated to industry and vocational training. Huxley feared that Arnold's efforts to protect a traditionalist education could thwart the nascent movement to admit natural and social sciences into the curriculum, and thereby perpetuate a purely literary education that would be both impractical and elitist. Both parties saw the future character of education as the future character of the nation and its citizens. In the end, each sought to resolve the questions: *How shall we live? What shall we become?*

The shorthand version of Arnold's fear was that the United Kingdom would become the United States—or at least his characterization of the United States—thereby trading the beauty and virtue of its honorable historical character for the chattels and conveniences of the State's youthful, superficial materialism. Education, in Arnold's view, is not only about cultivating skills to earn our daily bread, but also fostering an inwardness that sustains vision, courage, and beauty. And these virtues, he maintained, if they do not contribute directly to industry, contribute practically and invaluably to human flourishing. Moreover, these virtues, nurtured by poetry, art, and eloquence, sustain the work of social criticism, which in turn assists us in our reflection on such everyday issues as our conduct, the moral implications of scientific findings, and the social conditions of industry.[56] These virtues belong to a constellation of inward stars.

There exists, according to Arnold, a correlation between America's materialism and its constricted Puritan religiosity. He was convinced that in the U.S., the spiritual tends not to include art, literature, and other forms of beauty that awaken and challenge the spirit. Rather, the spiritual is identified almost exclusively with a literalistic, Biblical religion that is suspicious of (what Arnold called) culture. This is hardly an adequate account of the religious and cultural life in the U.S. Religiously, we are a diverse nation. Even if we *were* all Puritans—and we emphatically are not—that religious tradition is itself rich, plural, and hardly dismissive of the aesthetic. Nonetheless, I think Arnold's exaggerated diagnosis of what ails America—and his own industrialized Britain—reveals a very real, if subtle, cultural tumor. I suspect that "much of our present discomfort"—our missing sense of time and place, past and future, community and nationhood, purposefulness and cooperation—springs from a politics, an economics, an educational philosophy, and a spiritual perspective that is dangerously restrictive, severing us from various sources of life that would nurture us as individuals and as a nation. Arnold might remind us that if material acquisition is our national aspiration and utilitarianism our national philosophy, then we will surely become an obese yet morally malnourished people.

A few decades after Arnold published "Literature and Science," an American made a similar case, one as powerful and nuanced. W. E. B. Du Bois argued against Booker T. Washington's efforts to establish vocational schools for disenfranchised African Americans. Although Washington's mind and heart were earnestly invested in advancing the material and social circumstances of oppressed African Americans, Du Bois offered, to my mind, a more plausible avenue to freedom; namely, he proposed a more holistic educational program that was already available to white people of means.

For fourteen years I brought Vassar students to the Green Haven Correctional Facility, a maximum security prison in upstate New York. The students and I discussed with the inmates such issues as domestic violence, parenting, alternatives to violence, victim awareness, and the socioeconomic conditions of communities-at-risk. When I first traveled to Green Haven, I assumed it would be a one-time visit. I had been invited by my friend and colleague, Larry Mamiya, who was resolute in his efforts to build bridges of communication between Vassar and the prison. Like Larry, I kept going back—week after week, month after month, year after year. Often I wanted to quit. I was busy; some weeks I begrudged my four-hour appointment at the prison. But each week I returned.

I'm a university professor. I'm bookish. But aside from books, I have learned as much from my incarcerated teachers at Green Haven as from any other single source of learning.

Here I have also learned much about teaching, for some of the most skillful teachers I have ever encountered live within its high walls.

At Green Haven, I witnessed firsthand the cruel consequences of institutional racism. I am not referring to the prison itself, but to a nation that tolerates those socioeconomic conditions, known as crime-generative factors, directly linked to criminality. These familiar, calculable, preventable conditions make it statistically likely for a black child born into certain communities in and around New York City to end up incarcerated. Individuals are responsible for their specific crimes—I learned this in and out of prison. But so are nations. I learned this in prison.

I suppose the simplest reason I returned is this: The incarcerated are humans, and I would go to acknowledge their humanity. Humanity longs for humanity, theirs for mine and mine for theirs. It also longs for *the humanities*. This I have learned in the most tangible of ways. It is another lesson about the nature of education, not from the conservative Arnold nor from the radical Du Bois, but from the prisoners at Green Haven.

I recently received a letter from a Green Haven inmate, Carry Greaves. He sent me a collection of his poems, poems dedicated to "African-American women for their unyielding love, support, and contribution to the global community." I first met Mr. Greaves when he invited me to meet with a prison group that was discussing moral reasoning. Mr. Greaves asked if I could lead a session on Lawrence Kohlberg's and Carol Gilligan's theories on moral development. A year later I found myself in another discussion group with Mr. Greaves. This time the topic was the classical sociologist, Max Weber. The last time I met with Mr. Greaves and his fellow inmates, we discussed a collection of poems that pertained to environmental justice.

Poetry, moral philosophy, and sociology—such intellectual disciplines are not often associated with people behind bars. The common assumption is that the educational interests of incarcerated persons, insofar as there are any, are limited to vocational-technical training. That assumption is false. The incarcerated at Green Haven are starved for the nourishment of heart and mind that comes from philosophy, poetry, sociology, history, and art. I do not mean to understate their desire for practical, vocational skills. Still, maybe due to the bleakness of their environment, they truly understand that humans cannot flourish on bread and water alone. These men know, in ways tangible and terrible, that you can starve a man while feeding him. And so, even as their basic needs are met, the incarcerated have a hunger for life-enhancing wisdom, knowledge, and beauty.

In his essay, "Walking," Thoreau claimed that the swamp in his backyard is the most valuable part of his property—"the jewel" of the landscape.[57] Why lavish such praise on a quagmire? Because the swamp's value lies precisely in its lack of apparent utility. It is not susceptible to utilitarian ends, to the forces that would tame it, domesticate it, and make it serve profitable purposes. By its very nature, the swamp defeats utilitarian aspirations. It stands, rather, as a wild presence, a valuable reminder that many things in life transcend narrow, functional roles. Many of our greatest joys come from those people, places, creatures, and pursuits that are—from a utilitarian view—worthless. When we as a nation lose our capacity to celebrate swamps, we become less able to justify a liberal arts education that supports intellectual and artistic play, risk, and love. Let this lesson illuminate the university: human flourishing requires diverse nourishment.

On the last day of *It's Only Natural*, our class piled into two vans and drove northeast to Innisfree Garden, home to streams and waterfalls, terraces and cliffs, rocks and stones, plants and trees, herons and geese, all nestled around the forty-acre Lake Tyrrel.

Innisfree is designed to be experienced like an art gallery: room by room and in no particular order, with no focal point or central display. These intricate rooms of rock, plant, water, and sky have been described as cup gardens. Each room or cup defines an area—sometimes large, sometimes small—that brings together various natural elements in a design that may emphasize tension, motion, form, or space. At the same time, each garden intimates balance and harmony without formality or strict symmetry.

The inspiration for Innisfree comes from various traditions: a Chinese landscape philosophy that goes back to the eighth-century poet and painter, Wang Wei; an ancient Japanese landscape tradition that has its origins in the *Sensai Hisho*, the *Secret Garden Book*; and also, inescapably, a North American tradition of jazz-like garden rhythms. Finally, the inspiration for Innisfree comes from the native rocks, plants, trees, water, hills, and animals—that is, from the land itself.

Innisfree was the natural choice for the site of our last class meeting. During the semester, we had often probed the ambiguities of that very concept, *natural*. We noted the ways that so-called natural landscapes are invariably shaped by human activity. We also explored the ways that human activity itself can be considered natural, since humans, too, are natural creatures. Innisfree embodied a marvelous union of nature and culture, of non-human and human worlds pulling harmoniously together. Such harmony is not the single or most significant aspect of the "natural." But it was on this peaceable theme that we chose to end our course.

Another focus of the course was the exploration of various examples of American landscapes. For geographic and personal reasons, we studied at length the Hudson River School, with its emphasis on the interrelation between humans, nature, and spirituality. Hudson River School artists such as Thomas Cole, Frederick Edwin Church, and Asher Brown Durand understood landscape paintings not as pretty pictures designed to comfort or cheer us, but as powerful revelations with the capacity to stir us—and challenge us—aesthetically, morally, and spiritually. Their paintings often interweave the wild with the domesticated, suggesting a demanding moral ideal of the need for both feral and cultivated beauty in our lives and land. Walking in Innisfree is not unlike walking among the Hudson River School collection at the Metropolitan Museum of Modern Art in New York City. Yet perhaps Innisfree is a richer expression of the North American landscape, for it reflects both the vision of artists like Cole, Church, and Durand, and also the rich diversity of cultures that populate the American land. Innisfree's combination of Asian and Hudson River School inspirations allows for a fuller experience of a distinctively American land.

Furthermore, Innisfree inspires contemplation. Walk its paths and enter a quiet, thoughtful, meditative disposition. In this place, the connection between outer and inner, between sense and sensibility, is effortlessly present. For about an hour we walked individually and in small groups through the garden. When we reconvened, Paul gave the students instructions for a private, contemplative exercise that Lorain Fox Davis had assigned to us during our stay in Colorado. "Find a place that seems to speak to you in a distinctive way, ask it a question, and expect a response." Again, the students knew what to do. They had learned how to travel deeply without traveling far. Reading, writing, viewing, discussing, thinking, drawing, mapping, songwriting, dancing, walking, and contemplating—these practices, all used together, had become familiar to these students. Even their two professors had become somewhat accustomed to this course in search of itself.

❧

Where, then, does our *search for a university*—this broad exploration of the culture of the modern university, of its manners and methods, of its ideals and goals—leave Paul and me and our course? Neither of us had thought through the seminar's implications for our disciplines and for the broader university culture. We did understand, however, given the anomalous nature of our course—with its short contemplative exercises, its first day contra dance, its almost weekly field trips up and down the Hudson, its songwriting workshop with the Canadian music group, *Tamarack*, its three-hour session with Navajo Ben Barney who, among other things, asked each student to self-identify in terms of family and place—that we had better seek a curricular base for the course outside our home departments. In the end we decided it would be best to offer *It's Only Natural* through two nascent university departments that were themselves in search of an identity: Environmental Studies and American Culture. We never intended for our course to challenge prevailing trends in higher education, much less to give offense to colleagues in our own departments. Our focus, rather, was on developing a course that would challenge our students and ourselves. Better to concentrate on teaching our students than justifying a course to our peers.

It's Only Natural was, by all accounts, a successful course. A genuine community of learning was established. We came to trust each other with our questions, hopes, fears, and beliefs, seeing each other as travelers on a common journey. We deeply engaged with each other and with a rich variety of material, inside and outside the classroom. I'm tempted to call it an instance of transformative education. It certainly changed me. I will no doubt keep asking myself, "Can I really do *that* in class?" But I am now more likely to answer, "Yes, I can."

In "The American Scholar," Emerson argued that American colleges do best when they surpass convention and "gather from far every ray of various genius to their hospitable halls, and, by the concentrated fires, set the hearts of their youth on fire."[58] As an American scholar, I want to gather from far. As an American teacher, I want to set hearts on fire.

Part IV

Borne by a Course

Day Nine

Drive to Flagstaff

"Thy lot or portion of life is seeking after thee; therefore be at rest from seeking after it."[59]

—*Ralph Waldo Emerson quoting Caliph Alī ibn Abī Ṭālib*

On the morning of the ninth day of our journey, Paul and I had breakfast with Vida and Bill. The evening prior marked our final visit to Shiprock, when I, the clumsy pilgrim, had made myself too visible on the sacred mountain. Now, less conspicuously, the four of us would enjoy our last meal together and recount our recent impressions of the mountain. Once again, we ate at Riverwalk.

By then, we had eaten seven meals in Farmington, and *all* of them at the same restaurant. I wondered at this. With Farmington's abundance of dining options—Mexican, Thai, Chinese, barbeque, seafood restaurants, brewhouses, and even an Irish Cantina—why had we returned invariably to the same table? Whenever the topic of dining arose, Paul or Vida or Bill would say, "Why don't we eat at Riverwalk?" If I had been with my parents, I might have expected a meal or two at this restaurant, with its overwhelming innocuousness, its location adjacent to Farmington's Best Western hotel. But I was with an adventuresome poet, photographer, and sage. Were my dining companions members of an exotic cult who took the unsuspecting, perfectly ordinary Riverwalk as their meeting place?

Perhaps they were. Perhaps the name of the cult and its gathering place are one and the same: RIVERWALK, or Beholders of the Extraordinary. These cult members travel incognito. Except for that subtle intensity in their faces, they would go unnoticed walking down the street or dining out. They travel quietly, eat unassumingly, live unobtrusively. And they often adhere to routine, for they can find the extraordinary in the perfectly ordinary. Remember, it was Paul who initiated our lunches together at Vassar—each week on the same day, at the same time, in the same place. Had Paul initiated something more than lunch? Had he initiated *me* into this cult? Here I was, dining with his brethren at Riverwalk, participating in their cultic ritual.

Had I less discretion, I might have asked my companions: "Are you impressed by these large plastic menus?" "Are you keen on that 'Chicken Fried Steak' and 'Onion Thing'?" "Do you *like* this restaurant?" And if such questions were not gently ignored, I can imagine the responses:

> It is not a matter of like or dislike.
> This location is adequate.
> Much may be found here—in a face, in a spoken word, in a slant of light.[60]
> We have recently been to the Mountain. Isn't that enough?
> Must we add to it Thai barbeque?

Earlier in these pages I asked, "Why must our most authentic journeys be solitary and exotic?" I am beginning to understand now that revelation can occur anywhere, at any time, even there at Riverwalk. *Especially* at Riverwalk. After all, Riverwalk is where we live. Our days are mostly plain and ordinary, apportioned into routines and chores. Tedium, dullness, that "gray across the bridge"—these are the shape and color of life's building blocks, at least most of them. We can wish that it were otherwise, that each moment in our lives were charged with preternatural wonderment and awe, that the length of our lives extended in seamless, protracted bliss. Yet in the face of this wish we meet reality: Riverwalk. Spend enough time on that hundred-foot yacht or at the new Zen center, and you'll find that the most alluring inevitably becomes the most familiar. Empirically speaking, the ordinary is where we live. And it is wise to accept all this gray in our lives, as Paul's poem recommends. Accept that "it would be all right, with much still to praise."[61]

But what of extraordinary places like Shiprock? What of the occasional grandeur and brilliance and mystery of it all? And what of those tiny, wondrous events that make this life a little more manageable, more lovely? This, too, needs to be acknowledged—"gray, then, *with splashed color*"—and invited, and called upon. While revelation may not be our daily condition, we can cultivate an openness to it, a readiness for those moments when it breaks into our lives. True, some places and events like Shiprock tend to come crashing into our consciousness, transforming us regardless of our preparation. Yet grace usually approaches more subtly. It is vital that we pay attention and remain receptive to "the gray" and to the extraordinary that may appear within it—whether grand or slight, whether a mountain or a new penny.

Deirdre got the car. When she pulled it out of the driveway for the last time, crammed with pieces of our life together, the bright spring day was notably indifferent to the occasion. Our parting called for gray skies and melancholy fog; nature gave us sunshine and budding flowers. If I sought sympathy from the weather, I was disappointed. The sky would not commiserate.

That year, the seasons of my life did not match the spirit of either equinox: spring brought the end of a former life, and fall—blessed fall!—brought the hope of another. And not only hope. Fall brought me the life that holds me and loves me to this day.

Annie Dillard, my teacher and coach in so many things, understands the importance of paying attention to opportunities for grace. I would not be surprised to learn that she is a member of the Riverwalk cult, shaking gourds under plastic tablecloths at meetings. Dillard is at home in the ordinary. Still, she knows that "there are lots of things to see, unwrapped gifts and free surprises. The world is fairly studded with strewn pennies cast broadside from a generous hand."[62]

This is her good news: grace is embedded—implanted—in the world around us. It's there for the taking, for the seeing: *what you see is what you get.* But Dillard adds a warning: "It is dire poverty indeed when a man is so malnourished and fatigued that he won't stoop to pick up a penny." Dire, yes, but also common. And the way out of such poverty is as difficult as it is straightforward: "If you cultivate a healthy poverty and simplicity, so that finding a penny will literally make your day, then, since the world is in fact planted in pennies, you have with your poverty bought a lifetime of days." To have pennies in our lives, then, we must train. There are lots of exercises: open your eyes and try to see something, and see it well. Get outside. Take walks. Buy a bike. Ride it. Slow down. Look at the stars. Look at a friend or a stranger. Love him. Comfort her.

These exercises carry no guarantee. Our daily rituals and disciplined training cannot ensure that we will find "unwrapped gifts and free surprises." Grace may abound, but it remains a gift: it cannot be insisted on. Ultimately, grace must come to us from outside ourselves. When it comes, if it does, we must try to be awake.

In my search for a course, these lessons in gray and color proved vital. I am grateful for my education in Riverwalk. In the course of a life or a semester, there will always be much that is gray. I need to help my students accept this. In our wired and wireless world, students are endlessly plugging into kaleidoscopic digital displays. The classroom is no exception: glowing with cell phones, tablets, laptops, and projectors, it begins to resemble an Apple Store. It is no wonder that today's students are impatient with inanimate words on pages and professors at lecterns. But how are our students to see through all the synthetic color? How are they to learn? And if they become blinded by the artificial light, how can they trust the gray? How can they see the shine of pennies on the ground?

Perhaps the situation is not so grim. I have no complaint with color. I am no Luddite haranguing our Digital Age. But too much dazzle can be deceptive. Many of our students know this. Indeed, some are eager for a different kind of learning: quieter, slower, more thoughtful, more gray. Patient learning is not without its student constituency. On some days I think the sect is growing. Without exactly knowing it, many have quietly joined that "unending 'silent secret conversation,' the life of steadfast attention."[63] Without knowing it, they have become members of Riverwalk. And without *my* knowing it, they have covertly recruited me to help.

How am I to teach these patient students? How am I to help them to see and live in the gray if I myself am hesitant and ambivalent about embracing it? After all, I am the one who sped into the desert in search of a course, a shimmering revelation—in sky writing, preferably, but also with rainbows and maybe flood lights. I had been taught by the wise First People of this nation, by the sacred landscape, by the mountain. Who could doubt that I was prepared for a luminous epiphanic flash? My heart was ripe, my teachers spiritual, my environs numinous. What revelation did I see? What lessons were imparted?

My journey to answer these questions continued.

In late November, I traveled to Denver to give a lecture at the annual meeting of the American Academy of Religion. During the meeting, I called my cousin, Tom, to see if I could visit his family and perhaps a few other relatives while there. The next thing I knew, I found myself at Tom's house, where, to my great surprise, about twenty-five of my relatives had gathered to greet me. For the next four hours, I hugged and laughed with aunts and uncles, nieces and nephews, first and second cousins. The past season of trials and sadness gave way to warmth, tenderness, and a sense of belonging. The evening was redemptive.

Tom and I had agreed to meet the following day for lunch. During our meal, he asked me, "Mark, do you ever fly?" I knew that Tom was writing a book titled, *How To Lift Cars off Your Face: A Practical Guide for Living without Limits.* To this day, I am not sure if he was speaking literally or figuratively. Still, his question made me wonder about my own wings, folded for so long in resignation to gravity. For over a year I had been pinned down. Tom's gift to me was to pose the essential question about unused wings.

The very next day, back home in upstate New York, I opened Denise Levertov's *The Stream and the Sapphire* for my morning reading and encountered these lines:

> Our shoulders ache. The abyss
> gapes at us.
>
> When shall we
> dare to fly?[64]

To be open to love and its risks is to be willing to soar. My shoulders ached with the spur of unused wings. Denver had readied me for flight.

After taking leave of Bill and Vida at Riverwalk, Paul and I began our 275-mile drive from Farmington to Flagstaff. This time we took no shortcuts. We stayed on that smooth, wide highway that we had foolishly bypassed a few days earlier in lieu of the mountain pass to Lukachukai. This day's drive was uneventful—though perhaps the exquisite beauty of the Painted Desert was itself an event. This span of multihued, pastel sandstone and volcanic ash appeared too soft and delicate for the designation, "badlands." Of course appearance and reality, as we know, can vary vastly. The Lakota, who first named this arid terrain, "*Makhóšika,*" or "bad land," understood and dwelled in this world that I only gazed on at sixty miles an hour from an air-conditioned rental car. If I had had a more intimate and practical relation to this land, if I were there with a family and community attempting to live off the soil or cross it by foot, I would no doubt grasp the challenges of its sand, its steep slopes, its gullies and canyons that can fill suddenly with raging torrents. Perhaps I, too, would reach for a name like "*Makȟóšika*."

We headed northwest out of Farmington to Teec Nos Pos, then west to Mexican Water, and finally southwest along Highway 160 through Dennehotso, Monument Valley, Baby Rock, Rare Metals, and down to Tuba City—the Navajo Nation's largest community. It lies on the north side of Highway 160 with the Hopi town of Moenkopi directly opposite to the south. This area has long been the site of land disputes and political tension between the Navajo and the Hopi. It's a long, complicated history, with the U.S. government acting as a central player in the removal, incarceration, and murder of Navajos and Hopis, followed by successive and clumsy federal efforts to undo the damage. To this day there remain disputes between the Navajo and the Hopi, but for the most part they interact with respect and civility. They understand that for their communities to move forward and beyond the present trials and challenges, they need to achieve their own Navajo-Hopi accord independent of the U.S. government. Tuba City and Moenkopi stand, then, as twin monuments to past pain and future hope.

When I met her, shortly after my return from Denver, neither pain nor hope was on my mind. The afternoon weather hardly foretold good fortune. It was misty, gray, and cold on that early December day. I had just checked my mail at the Vassar post office and was walking up the pathway back to my office in Blodgett Hall. She was walking down the path in the other direction. I say "fate"—she says "chance"—led us to that same spot at that same time.

It began rather simply: I saw her face on the path, and it commanded my complete attention. As she traveled past me, I turned and said, without thinking, "Your name is…." She stopped, looked into my eyes, and said confidently, "You don't know my name, but your name is Mark." I learned her name, *Mina*, and we talked of the insignificant—the weather, the time of day, the crushing flow of work. When we shook hands in parting, she did not blush when I held on too long.

Tuba City and Moenkopi are dusty and dry (literally and figuratively; no alcohol is available). Most travel guides say the towns are rundown and "empty." In Tuba City, some tourists occasionally stay at the Quality Inn as a stopover between the "movie sites" of Monument Valley and the Grand Canyon. The main attraction in town is the Tuba City Trading Post with its souvenirs and Indian crafts. The main attraction out of town, five miles to the west, are dinosaur tracks: two-hundred-million-year-old footprints of the half-ton *dilophosaurus.*

Such mammoth creatures seem emblems of survival. Dinosaurs endured for about one hundred fifty million years, almost four hundred times as long as *Homo sapiens* have existed. Still, it makes me wonder. To come so far and finally die out. For a modest tip, Navajo guides lead tourists in and around the maze of tracks. Who today guides us in the footprints of past Navajo? And who, in time to come, will guide future generations in the tracks of an extinct white North America? The Navajo? Some species descended from ours*?* Or only sedges and insects growing and crawling in our footprints? Isolated, dusty, and brown, Tuba City poses such questions, though the answers it offers are not encouraging.

The Navajo name for Tuba City is *Tó Naneesdizí*, the "tangled waters." That's a good description of Tuba City's history. In 1870 the Hopi Chief *Toova* converted from one Native American religion to another, from the Hopi Way to Mormonism.

Two years later, Mormons founded Tuba City across from Moenkopi. People often think of deserts as empty, but they are full of—some might say fraught with—religion. Years later, a different kind of religion filled this area: the credo of the Cold War's nuclear arms race, which led to the production of hundreds of uranium mines in the Southwestern desert. Uranium was unearthed, bombs were built and stockpiled, and Tuba City became a central office for the Rare Metals Corporation and the Atomic Energy Commission.

All in all, about 3.9 million tons of uranium were dug up from 1944 to 1986. The U.S. government was the consumer, private mining companies the producers, and Native Americans, once again, the exploited. The Navajo miners, who were in desperate need of employment, were neither provided any protective gear nor told of known health risks. Moreover, without their knowledge or consent, they became the subjects of medical investigations on radiation exposure. When the mines shut down as the Cold War thawed, fences and other basic precautions against the dangers of nuclear debris failed to go up. To this day, piles of radioactive waste and miles of open tunnels and pits deface tribal lands, and radioactive dust carried by desert winds contaminates Navajo, Hopi, and Mormon communities, among others. In the Navajo Nation alone, there are over 1,000 abandoned uranium mines. No wonder the Navajo named uranium, *leetso*, yellow dirt, which, to their ears, sounds like a reptilian monster.[65]

What will become of "Tangled Waters"? Extinction and extermination are in its past, and even the optimist might predict the same for its future—a final (radioactive?) obsolescence on the level of Cretaceous-Tertiary extinction. Or perhaps Tuba City can offer the world some encouragement, something like hope. After all, the Navajo and the Hopi still endure in spite of past atrocities and present obstacles. The genocide of Native Americans is among the most terrible in human history. Their abuse is proof of human cruelty, yet their survival and resilience are evidence of human strength and courage. Tuba City reminds us that the dark wind of destruction need not always prevail.

This brings me to another of Tuba City's offerings. It is home to Sergeant Jim Chee, the famous Tuba City Navajo tribal policeman of Tony Hillerman's *The Dark Wind.* While confronting the fury of the dark wind, Sgt. Chee exhibits steadfastness, honesty, ingenuity, and courage. Perhaps Tuba City does have much to offer the world. But for Paul and me, on our long road trip from Farmington to Flagstaff, this place of Hopi and Navajo, of dinosaurs and Mormons, of uranium and Sgt. Chee, of tangled waters and dark wind—this place is a small dot on the Budget Rental road map: a place to refuel, to eat a late lunch, to move on from without delay. After pumping gas at the Tuba City Express, we dined on tortillas, Swiss potato soup, and milkshakes at Kate's Café, just across the dusty road from the Trading Post.

Within minutes of meeting Mina, I was back in my office, inviting her to coffee over email:

> Have you read much Robert Frost? This morning I came upon these lines, and they reminded me of my own need on occasion to be *derailed*:
>
> Bless you, of course you're keeping me from work,
> But the thing of it is, I need to be kept.
> There's work enough to do—there's always that;
> But behind's behind. The worst that you can do
> Is set me back a little more behind.
> I shan't catch up in this world, anyway.
> I'd rather you'd not go unless you must.[66]
>
> I'm starting to think we all must go. But it's good to be "set back," too. Let's set each other back, together, over coffee.

On that day, I was separated but still married, and, as I soon learned, Mina was officially engaged. Yet, when our worlds collided, each was knocked out of its orbit. Soon, my divorce was filed, her engagement called off, our courses "set back," perhaps, but also thrust brilliantly in a new direction. Untethered from our suns, we spun madly around each other. One thing was sure: I was flying.

Days Ten through Twelve

The ASLE Conference

On day ten Paul and I woke up in Flagstaff, home to Northern Arizona University. The university was hosting the biennial meeting of the *Association for the Study of Literature and the Environment* (ASLE), and Paul and I were to give an academic paper on the team-taught course that we had yet to teach, on material that we had yet to comprehend. As we approached Flagstaff from the north on the previous day, traveling on Highway 89 through the Navajo Nation, down past Cameron, Gray Mountain, Wupatki, and into the Coconino National Forest, I thought about how the character of our Southwest trip would soon change. Entering an academic conference always feels a bit like walking into a straitjacket. There is a fair amount of posturing, name-dropping, jargon, and papers read too fast in prose too dense. The expansive, quiet, vivid desert was soon to be replaced by the crowded, muggy, boisterous lecture hall. In fairness to ASLE, I should say that the conference turned out better than most. I learned much from the various sessions and conversations and displayed books. But these lessons differed considerably from those of the desert.

It was for good reason that I sensed impending change. I knew that Paul and I would see little of each other at the conference. We would each have our own colleagues to meet, sessions to attend, book exhibits to peruse, and so on. This was how it should be. Still, drawing near to Flagstaff, it began to occur to me that the greatest gift the desert gave me may have been an even broader, deeper friendship with Paul.

I now better understand the connection between what I had

thought of as a private, solitary search for my life and a joint, shared search with Paul for course material. The connection, complex at it is, seems so obvious to me now: Paul's friendship was central to both searches. This is not to belittle what I learned from Lorain, Ben, the Clifts, and the land itself. But the foundation of the Vassar course, I now realize, was not the texts or the topics or the field trips. It was a friendship. The friendship predicated the way we read the texts, saw the sights, engaged with the students. And it was the friendship that profoundly nurtured and supported me in my own personal search; in the desert, yes, but also upon my return to the Hudson River Valley.

On day twelve, however, the desert had still another lesson for me. Happily, the ASLE programmers had scheduled daily fieldtrips into the diverse communities in and around Flagstaff. On this warm Thursday, a group of us traveled to a hogan in the desert where six Navajo women would discuss their experiences of this land, as well as the efforts of private companies and the federal government to remove them from it. Of all the things I remember about this remarkable visit, it is how these women spoke their names at the beginning of the event.

It was a simple thing, really—what we usually call an introduction. One by one, these women offered their names and those of their home lands. It is easy not to pay close attention to introductory comments, and most of the guests were feeling groggy after the long, dry trip through the desert. We had attended academic sessions for the last two days and had all heard at least forty introductions already: "Welcome Professor So-and-So from such-and-such university whose expertise is in this-and-that." Here we found ourselves again, at the introductory phase of yet another ASLE program. But this time, in the desert, something different happened.

It came forcefully, through the simple and honest act of each woman announcing her name and place name. "*Hello. My name is.... My family and people are from the land of....*" It was that simple.

This is who I am and where I come from. Their voices had gravity, their names had power. They did not speak hurriedly, but with deliberation and care. As guests, we immediately grasped the profound self-knowledge and sense of place that were communicated in these acts of self-identification. It was as if we had been led out of conferencing and into a sacred place. I had the distinct sense of meeting my teachers. If I could emulate to a modest degree these placed and displaced Navajo women, practice their confidence and grounded bearing, then perhaps I, too, might learn to speak my name. I might make headway on my course.

During the week between returning from Denver and meeting Mina on the path, I recorded in my journal:

> Religion is, as it were, the calm bottom of the sea at its deepest point, which remains calm however high the waves on the surface may be.[67]

Wittgenstein always *idealized* religion; that is, he wrote about religion at its best, not its worst. Still, his statement about religion is a good depiction of the inner calm that I had been attempting to achieve with such aids as Paul, my bees, the woods, and, yes, religion (of a roughly Transcendentalist, panentheistic, Unitarian sort). Equanimity, steadiness, self-possession: these were the virtues toward which I had aspired and made progress. And just in time, too, for such virtues would help steady me as I braved a new tempest—my courtship with Mina. Eighteen months before, the "perfect storm" had submerged and drowned me; this new storm would overpower and eventually elevate me.

I recall the drama of it all with some chagrin: incessant breakups and reconciliations, clothes hanging in other's closets or thrown out on doorsteps, heavy drinking, passionate sex, alternatingly romantic and furious text messages, sparring and screaming one minute, laughing and rolling on the floor the next. Chaos theory made flesh—that was our early courtship. My life was mightily rocked and undeniably buoyed by Mina's beauty—physical and spiritual.

Is it possible that I liked the chaos, even sought it out after my languid former marriage? Absolutely not. I would have run from it under any circumstances—*particularly* after the collapse of my marriage—had it not been for Mina's beauty and for my own preternatural confidence in us. Looking back, I am surprised by the calm with which I met the chaos. I remember, for example, the tumultuous day that Mina managed to break up with two men, her fiancé and me. In the face of such turmoil, I remember talking to her calmly, asking about her work schedule and inquiring about her dinner plans. Even then, I felt somehow assured—perhaps recklessly—in a vision of who we could become and of where we could go together. The exact route was indirect and often as dangerous as the Lukachukai passage, yet with Frost I could say:

> Oh, come forth into the storm and rout
> And be my love in the rain.[68]

Not long after returning from the Southwest to the Hudson River Valley, I walked home from Vassar one evening and encountered a deer on a trail in the woods. When we saw each other, we both froze—I with delight, the deer with fright. Next the deer lowered its head and stomped the ground twice with its right front hoof. I did likewise, stomping twice. After a short pause, the deer stomped again, and again I imitated. We went on like this for some time, responding to each other. Was this a rare moment of intimate communion between two distinct creatures, deer and human, as we each made our way in this tiny, shared corner of this vast, lonesome world? I know better. The deer, alarmed, was only doing its best to ward me off.

Still, in a world in which humans find themselves desperate to communicate with something or someone nonhuman in the natural world, I felt some satisfaction that the deer and I had responded to each other, had exchanged a dialogue of stomps. Not wanting to cause the deer any further worry, I turned slowly away and began walking up the trail, imagining its eyes on my back, its nose on my scent, both of us going our own ways, both traversing the same land, moving with purpose, desiring food, shelter, and safety. I headed home to eat while the deer, foraging here and there, was already at home feeding.

For some time, I had been deliberately cultivating a sense of place, a home, in the Hudson River Valley. I had some friends, some community, and some knowledge of the history, cultures, and geology of my place. Still, I could not set aside the notion that the deer belonged to their place more naturally, more assuredly, than I ever would. I returned from the desert with a renewed desire to put down roots—roots so deep that I would stop needing to look for them. Yet I also returned with an educated suspicion that such an unselfconscious sense of belonging would never be mine. Looking back in my journal recently, I was surprised to read that I had considered returning to the tradition of my childhood, of "my people": the Greek Orthodox Church. I desired history, ancestors, and traditions. If I could not join the Navajo and the deer, I thought, then perhaps I could rejoin my fellow Greeks.

This alone indicates the depth of my yearning to be connected to something that is part of me yet larger than me, that could contain me as the land enfolds Shiprock and its people. Yet such attempts to become something that in fact we aren't—something that never was or is no longer native to us—feel artificial and futile. Wittgenstein understood the psychological vanity of such longing when he wrote:

> Tradition is not something a man can learn; not a thread he can pick up when he feels like it; any more than a man can choose his own ancestor. Someone lacking a tradition who would like to have one is like a man unhappily in love.[69]

I was a man unhappily in love—that is, in love with that which could never be mine: the sense of belonging naturally to a place and its tradition with unquestioning ease and affection.

I see things differently now. I must start from where I am, growing in my own place. My people are not the deer. They are not the Navajo. Nor are they the Greeks of my parents' Orthodox tradition. Oh, I am related in various ways to the deer, the Navajo, and the Greeks. But they are not my tribe. I must cultivate my garden and not attempt transplantation in someone else's. All gardens need to be tilled now and then. The soil becomes compressed and loses its fertility unless it is turned over and renewed with fresh, organic material. Without a measure of the wild, a garden becomes lifeless.

My courtship with Mina brought a generous measure of the wild. "The wildness of the savage," Thoreau wrote, "is but a faint symbol of the awful ferity with which good men and lovers meet."[70] I don't know about Thoreau's savage, but I now know firsthand about the "awful ferity with which lovers meet." Life teems with feral experiences. Control is not an option. Uncertainty reigns supreme. And so Andre Breton's dictum, "Hardly anyone dares to face with open eyes the great delights of love." Yet how was I to close my eyes in the presence of Mina? Even if we tremble before the wild beauty, it transfixes us. With eyes open, then, I embraced the wild and came alive. This was Mina's greatest gift to me.

In wildness, it is useless to attempt to master one's environment, including one's intimate relationships. When we relinquish control over what is wild, we accept, too, the autonomy and distance of the lover. Honoring and not lamenting this distance is a form of respect and even of love. Rilke must have had something like this is mind when he wrote:

> Once the realization is accepted that even between the closest human beings infinite distances continue to exist, a wonderful living side by side can grow up, if they succeed in loving the distance between them which makes it possible

> for each to see the other whole and against a wide sky![71]

It was Mina who, implicitly, insisted on "distance" as a form of respect and love. With her help, I learned to step back and allow space. With this perspective we could appreciate each other, "whole and against the wide sky." In contrast, Deidre, with my help, had sought to obliterate the distance, yet all the while endeavoring to conceal herself. This measure of distance, in part, distinguished my new life from my former.

I used to ask my Vassar students, *Do you know where you will grow old and die?* Unfair question! Many of these students were barely eighteen years old. After a few seconds of silence and many looks of bewilderment, I would proclaim triumphantly that I would grow old and die in the Hudson River Valley. Such confidence! Such self-knowledge! I understand now the hubris and arrogance in this reply to my own question. Who can claim to know the future with any certainty? Whose life is subject to such control? In those days I still thought that I could largely plot and pilot my course. In retrospect, I would have liked to say to my students something like this:

> Do you ever think about where or what is your home? Have you ever considered the option of settling down, of staying put, of genuinely knowing a place and caring for it? Have you ever considered adopting Poughkeepsie as your home, of letting it adopt you as one of its own? This will be your place for many years. Why not count yourself as a citizen of this valley? My own hope is that I will grow old and die here, that as my body has worked and loved this land, that in my death my flesh and my bones will join the valley's dirt and stone and water. Yet this hope is accompanied by the knowledge that plans are but predictions and not assured outcomes. My hope for you and me, then, is that wherever we are, we may learn to love a

> place and call it home, may learn to speak our name and the name of our land.

In time, the chaos of our courtship subsided even as much of the wild remained. Clothes stayed on their hangers. Quarrels abated. The drinking moderated. The passion, however, still flamed. It was all rather miraculous. Two years after meeting Mina on that path, and exchanging one violently disruptive storm for another, I seemed to have had landed on my feet—albeit running, panting, and a bit lightheaded. I was grounded enough, evidently, to write the following in my journal:

> Tonight with friends we sang carols. After the singing, we all gathered in a circle and spoke of things for which we were grateful. I spoke of friends and family, yet my mind inwardly thought *Mina*—force, grace, and practicality in motion. Seeing her in the circle this Christmas Eve, I knew she was my first love. I hoped she'd be my last.

On Easter Sunday, I proposed to her. It was a brilliant morning as we woke up and got ready to go to a friend's house for lunch. Mina looked entirely stunning. I thought, could I really ask *her* to marry me? Then again, how could I *not*? For the proposal, I didn't go down on bended knee, nor did I present a ring. Instead, I baked her what turned out to be the world's ugliest chocolate cake and presented a pair of diamond earrings, as per my mother's suggestion. When Mina opened the box, I reached for her hand and asked for it, too. She said yes. In that moment, in my beating heart, I knew I had come home.

Where am I today? Have I learned to speak my name? What place do I call home? Today, as I write in the backyard of Mina's parents' house in Seattle, I am revisiting that unfair question that I posed to my Vassar students. We are visiting Seattle, in part, so that our seven-year-old daughter and three-year-old twins can spend time with their grandparents and cousins. We live in Providence, Rhode Island, and I teach at Brown University.

Talk about changes! Talk about plans altered! Talk about surprised by joy! The vital statistics have dramatically changed: divorce, marriage, children, home, career. At the very moment when I was searching hardest for a course, a complete constellation of life events was on its way to collide with me, to pull me into its orbit, to change my life forever.

Upon impact, many of my most pressing problems and questions seemed to disintegrate. If I had *solved* them, this would be a different book, one providing handy, clear-cut answers to life's problems. Instead, I have mostly roamed from question to question, from doubt to inquiry and back again—and now to a rather sudden resolution. Yet perhaps the questioning and doubting were part of the homecoming. From troubled waters came restorative *contact*—intimacy with a partner, a friend, a child, a community, a place, Spirit. Such contact provided opportunities to love and to be loved, to accept and to be accepted, to celebrate life without denying its pain, to admit difficult times without despair, to carry on the search without being consumed by it, and to find those limited but indispensable crossings to safety. Relationships often bring pain, for intimacy can wound deeply. Yet they also help us to bear pain. *The ways of life that bring the most grief—intimacy and affection—are the very ones that we most need, that are our salvation.* It is tempting to pray to be spared from this exacting redemption. But we must resist that prayer. We would trade too much life for protection from pain. Rather, with John Donne we pray, "That our affections kill us not, nor dye."[72]

Our wish, then, should not be for a love or way that exempts us from pain, but instead for one that acknowledges pain as central to our experience. Not for a love or way that protects us from all wounds, but instead one that offers some healing for our inevitable wounds. And to say that pain is central to human experience is not to deny that joy is as well. "It would be all right, with much still to praise."

Exponential change followed my proposal to Mina on Easter Day. Over the next ten weeks, we sold the home in Poughkeepsie, bought a home in Providence, resigned from Vassar, got married, and boarded a plane to Australia for our honeymoon. That's a lot of change.

We left everything behind—or almost everything. Remember how Ben Barney, when traveling to Germany, left behind his language, family, traditions, and nation? Mina and I became that man waiting for the train, discarding all our baggage. Beds and blankets, desks and books, dressers and clothes, DVD player and microwave, pictures and rugs, every kitchen utensil, plate, cup, and fork: we abandoned it all. House, Vassar, friends, *history*—all left behind. What did I keep? Paul, the Walkers, my colleague Larry Mamiya and his family, and, insofar as I could, my memories of the land.

Mina perhaps left behind the most. It's a brave and difficult decision for a Korean immigrant to relinquish a secure academic position at a prestigious place like Vassar. Yet the move from Poughkeepsie was Mina's idea and desire. Her job was becoming increasingly joyless, and a "fresh start" increasingly promising. I followed her lead because I loved her, not because I grasped the wisdom of leaving it all behind. But now I understand. There are seasons of change that we must accept, even embrace. For better or worse, exponential change is never far from our everyday journey.

Day Thirteen

Field Trip to the Grand Canyon

Whose place is the Grand Canyon and who can name it? Is it as the Hopi call it, *Ongtupqa,* "Holy site"? Is it as the one-armed American explorer John Wesley Powell named it, "Grand"? Those who have seen it seem to agree that the six-million-year-old, mile-deep, 277-mile-long canyon resists being named. (To call it "holy" or "grand" is, in a sense, to forego a particular name.) As the Colorado River sinks and the Colorado Plateau rises, two billion years of the planet's history is revealed. The revelation of that history can bring the most cynical observer to sublime tears. I've seen it.

In the bus chartered by the organizers of the ASLE conference, the person beside me prepared me for the Grand Canyon as only an academic can. It was a ninety-minute ride from Flagstaff to the South Rim, but it felt much longer. The professor on my right made sure I understood the relation between tourism, post-industrialism, and the commodification of landscapes. It turns out that the Romantics, feeling acute competition with the agents of the Industrial Age, attempted to accrue some social capital by becoming experts in their own distinctive enterprise—the manufacturing of beauty and the sublime. The Romantics, I was told, sold the sublime in works of art to an uncouth middle class hungry for the status that accompanies culture and education. I was assured that the only way to *escape* the spell of the wild and its beauty was to interrogate its bourgeois history. I could hardly wait.

And then, in the middle of this private lecture, the brilliant and ineffable Grand Canyon suddenly loomed out the bus window: a staggering wilderness of rock and light rising from the land in one organic surge. A deep silence filled the bus. After that, I didn't hear another word from the professor on my right about producers and consumers of wild beauty.

Later, I asked the bus driver if he, too, had heard the silence. He had. He hears it most times as he approaches the rim of the canyon with his busloads of noisy tourists—groups of retirees, children, lawyers, Pentecostals, cooks, and academics, among others. Apparently, the wild is being widely consumed nowadays. Or more likely, the wild oversteps those who would trade in it—whether they are artists attempting to replicate it or academics working to deconstruct it. Don't get me wrong—I am glad that some artists are still aspiring to wild beauty, and I am willing to learn from scholars who seek to trace its genealogy. But I cannot believe that art and criticism can exhaustively represent, measure, analyze, or otherwise capture a place or event like this Canyon. The Grand Canyon resists our names. The bus turns a corner and our representations, however skillful, bow to the view out the window.

And this can happen at anytime, anywhere. On a bus to the Grand Canyon? Sure. But also on a bus through the canyons of New York City or along the canals of New Orleans. We need not travel to the Grand Canyon to learn that the view from our window is often larger than the art or theory that attempts to capture it. This is not to say that art and theory are necessarily less real or astonishing than the world around us. Not at all. Art and theory contribute to our world; they are part of it. They can even participate in the wild and add their own quality and insight to the land and to our lives. Yet art and theory can also obstruct our sight and insight. We can be held captive by a narrow, highly domesticated theory or picture of the world—natural and social—and thereby become blind to its vast intricacies, subtleties, complexities, and mysteries.

After a three-hour hike from the rim of the Grand Canyon toward the river and back, just far enough to experience significant shifts in temperature, the group reconvened and traveled by bus to an isolated site directly on top of the South Rim. As often happens at camp, our group of disparate individuals began to bind together. Delicious tacos, gorgeous landscape, and lovely weather all conspired to make us instant friends. We ate heartily, talked energetically, and laughed easily.

But the Canyon once again commanded our attention. This time we were summoned by a sunset streaming in and over and beyond the Canyon's walls. It probably lasted for thirty minutes, yet it seemed longer. Behind all the schools of thought, the Grand Canyon shored. All conversation stopped—who would speak at such a moment? The group disbanded. We were individuals again, scattered along the rim, contemplating in silence and solitude the grandeur of the Grand Canyon.

Birth and death are Canyon-like, for they, too, ground our experiences of reality, taking us more deeply into ourselves as we reckon with those forces outside us.

At the ten-week checkup, Mina and I anxiously peered at the ultrasound screen, searching for the lively heart. Just a week prior we had heard it thumping at about 175 beats per minute. Yet on this day, the screen showed no flicker in the chest, no palpitation in the tiny body's shadowed form. Stillborn. Still life. *Morte natural*, once again. When my first marriage suddenly collapsed, my grief was dark and cold: the dying felt entirely unnatural. When the fetus died, my grief was white and hot: the death burned as terribly and naturally as wildfire. We grieved deeply. Our hearts blistered.

Day Fourteen

Drive from Flagstaff to Phoenix by Way of Sedona, Fly Back to New York

I woke up feeling wistful on day fourteen. It was the last day of our Southwest trip. I suppose I was mourning in advance my departure from the desert land. At the time, I did not understand how much of the desert I would keep.

I used to travel with few expectations of discovery, wonder, or mystery. It's different now. I now expect that something will happen. And not only when I travel. I frequently find myself waking up with an expectation that on this day something of importance will occur, if I am open to it. I admit it. Since the Southwest trip, I have become more expectant. I am working on staying awake. This is of course an ongoing undertaking. To help me, I recall a Rumi poem (or prayer) which repeats the refrain, *Don't go back to sleep*. I recite it every morning. I know how easy it can be to doze through life.

About eight months after the miscarriage, Mina and I once again searched the face of an ultrasound, beseeching life. This time there was motion: limbs, blood, and heart all stirred! The pregnancy progressed, joy and anxiety commingled with the exhaustive and variable information from the checkups, and then, at thirty-six weeks, a child—our Sabine—was born. Easter may be a symbol of hope and renewal, but Sabine—that wild, vigorous, formidable infant—was no symbol. She *was* new life. I held Easter incarnate in my hands and heart. But here's the mystery of it: I, too, was held.

After all these years since the Southwest trip, I still endeavor to wake up every morning ready to find splashes of color among the pervasive gray. Perhaps this is because of what I consider to be the miracle of my own new life. The desert helped me to find my name: "Mark of the Resurrection."

Of course I didn't know any of this on that last day of my Southwest trip. I had not yet been found by my new life, and moreover, I was simply too close to it all. We never know which guests will depart with us until we leave the party. I had assumed that when my Southwestern search was over, I would leave the company of the desert.

Captain García López de Cárdenas was searching for Cibola, one of the fabled Seven Cities of Gold. Instead, his Hopi guides led him to the edge of *Ongtupqa*—the Grand Canyon—and he thereby became the first known European to gaze upon it. Knowing the captain was seeking gold, the Hopi guides ushered him there to the bright yellow sunset on that Autumn day in 1540. Surely they thought, having seen *Ongtupqa,* the captain's search for gold and all other fantasies could come to an end. And perhaps the Hopi were right. I left many fantasies behind in the Canyon and elsewhere in the desert. What I didn't know back then was that once we've seen and acquired sight for real gold—for that which truly nourishes us—our longing for it grows.

Journal Entry: 17 June (Father's Day, my first one)

Last night around 3:00 a.m. I went to Sabine to comfort her. As I held her on my lap and kissed the fingers on her left hand, one at a time, her head tipped back and she fell asleep. And there we sat, Sabine sound asleep and I awake, holding her hand in a state of awe and wonder. For the next thirty minutes or so, I reflected on painful times in my life. I wanted to juxtapose those memories to the joy embodied on my lap. I wanted to remind myself, in the most tangible way, that joy does follow pain.

Then I started to wonder how I was going put her in the crib without waking her—always a challenge. But she herself leaned to the left and I found myself cradling her up in my arms. When I looked down at her, what did I see? The face of God. With her eyes closed, aimed directly at my own, her face shined like the moon, like a reflection and revelation of God. I didn't forget her frailty and mortality. But I did see God. When does our mother's face cease to be God's, and our child's take its place?

On the morning of the last day of the Southwest trip, I woke up planning my journey from Flagstaff to Phoenix, where I would catch a plane back to New York. I would ride to Phoenix with Dan Peck, another Vassar colleague attending the ASLE conference. The drive with Dan would be a compensatory joy during my departure from the desert. An admirable community and program builder, Dan had published two lovely books, one on Henry Thoreau and the other on James Fenimore Cooper. And at the time of the Southwest trip, he was working on a book about Asher B. Durand, one of the leading landscape artists who helped to define the Hudson River School. Dan and I would have much to talk about.

We headed south out of Flagstaff along the narrow and winding 89A to Sedona, then took 179 through Big Park and Oak Creek, and finally picked up I-17, making quick progress to Phoenix. It was a drive fraught with variance: ultra-rich lush resorts, developments, and country clubs against dry, austere landscapes. And then there was the contradiction of Metro Phoenix, with its "Brown Cloud" air pollution hovering over its florescent green lawns. The story of how over four million people came to live in this desert metro is, in part, a narrative about Americans choosing to settle and citify without consent from the natural world. It is nothing less than astonishing that one of the largest cities in the country takes as its home the Sonoran Desert, where the average high temperatures for five months of the year are over 100 °F. Yet with the air conditioner roaring, who's going to step outside? We live where we want to live—inside, with climate control.

And that's exactly where Dan and I were as we drove from Flagstaff to Phoenix—inside, with the air conditioning on high. I don't remember getting out of the car once. Of course, we had planes to catch, schedules to keep. My agenda for that day was more precise than any other during the last two weeks, a clear sign that I was exiting the desert time zone. A search for a course becomes less plausible when each moment of our lives is tightly scheduled for optimal performance, calculated for maximum yield. In the desert time zone (not to be confused with official U.S. Mountain Time) we encounter the opposite challenge. With all that open land, we respond by becoming increasingly resistant to all schedules and commitments. We begin to believe in the openness, the infiniteness, of time. We may forget about important things like meetings and promises. Perhaps that's part of the story behind the broken marriages of that spiritual Wild West town, Crestone, Colorado. Perhaps too much opportunity for revelation can drive us out of ordinary responsibility and into giddy unreliability, or worse.

Maybe it was my time to leave. Maybe it would have been dangerous for me to remain much longer in desert-time. Ben and Lorain were native to the desert and knew how to live there. I was a visitor, an amateur. Besides, like Robert Frost in the woods, I had promises to keep. As the day went on, I became increasingly accepting of the necessity of my departure. Though Dan had no idea how much he helped me, his informed, lively, and engaging conversation on what most would consider narrow academic topics was an immense pleasure. Without knowing it, Dan had prepared me for reentry to my Vassar life.

Day One Hundred

Back at Vassar

Reentry is the term academics use to refer to their return to campus life after a sabbatical. But what they really mean is *reversion*: the glow of the sabbatical is extinguished about five minutes into the first faculty meeting. What, then, am I to call my return to campus after journeying in the desert? *Digestion*—that's apt. While I was handling life's logistics in Poughkeepsie, I was still absorbing the desert. And I needed to work out how to integrate the Navajo desert with the Poughkeepsie suburbs. It was as if my heart and lungs were *circulating* this question of integration deeply and quietly beneath my conscious life. My body needed to take stock of what had happened in the desert, to adapt its new shape to its old home. While that occurred, I was paying late bills, ordering books for the fall semester, finishing up an article for submission, and building new chicken coops—I was taking care of business. Once a day, however, I allowed myself a thirty-minute walk dedicated to the question, *What did I bring back?* As this exercise was not especially satisfying, I gave it up after only two weeks. I was trying, once again, to find answers to questions the way I might solve a mathematical problem set. The gifts and challenges of the desert would not conform to this approach. I would need to be content to digest unconsciously.

On day one hundred, however, digestion would not be good enough. For on that day, Paul and I were called before the committee that was to fund our Southwest trip. Not unreasonably, the committee members wanted to know what we had learned. They wanted to know what we had brought back from the desert to offer to the College. I was ready to cooperate—to appease by offering satisfying accounts of our research trip. I was not going to be disingenuous, just selectively obliging. Paul, however, was obdurate and uncooperative. Keep in mind, we were not justifying to the committee how we had used its funds; we were asking for reimbursement. If this meeting didn't go well, Paul and I could be out a couple thousand dollars. But Paul visibly bristled as the committee asked such sensible questions as: "What lessons did you learn?" "What were some of the teaching techniques employed by the two Native American teachers?" "Which of these techniques and lessons will you use in the Vassar classroom?"

These committee members were pleasant colleagues. Their committee provided funding to bring a variety of alternative pedagogical approaches to campus. If there was ever a group to fund our kooky trip to the Southwest, this was it. Yet there stood Paul, stubbornly against them. He was not about to disclose the ways of our Native American teachers, for, in his mind, this was to dishonor a trust and, in a sense, to exploit Navajo and Lakota culture. In the end, he silenced this inquisitive committee. They backed off and we received our check.

I appreciate Paul's skillful reticence during this polite inquisition. Perhaps the committee learned something from him on that day. But still I ask, what did we bring back to Vassar, *for* Vassar? On one hot afternoon, while Paul and I had been scaling a dangerously steep slope at Shiprock, we had reflected on how risky the educative journey can be. As educators, risk-taking means asking real questions in the classroom—questions that sustain honest inquiry, questions to live by, questions to which we don't know the answers in advance. Students recognize real questions and they share in the intellectual wonderment when such inquiry leads to unexpected places. This element of *surprise*—of grace—is at the heart of honest, lively education.

When professors themselves are surprised and delighted, students sense that they are genuine participants in an intellectual journey.

This journey can lead to something like transcendence, not in a metaphysical, mystical sense, but in a practical, tangible one. While on the educational journey, we have the opportunity to transcend who we are—our old selves—and become somewhat new. We may encounter something astonishing that we cannot adequately capture in our current conceptual schema, and such astonishment may, on occasion, invoke in us something like reverence.

I am drawing on a religious vocabulary to describe this journeying—*transcendence, grace, new self, astonishment, reverence*—not because I consider education to be a type of religion, but because I consider religion, at its best, to be a type of education, a transformation of the self. This religious vocabulary highlights a dimension of education that is seldom mentioned amid all the talk of lesson plans, instructional objectives, and learning outcomes. *Transformation* was central to the education that Paul and I received in the desert, and it became a central—though unspoken—part of our team-taught course. And how am I to speak about *that*—about the unspoken—to a college committee? But perhaps I should try.

Not long after my journey into the desert, I was a Carnegie Scholar in the Higher Education Scholars Program. This entailed, among other things, three two-week residencies at the Carnegie Foundation, located in the foothills behind Stanford University, the same semiarid foothills I grew up in. During these residencies, I would take long walks into the hills among the cows, sometimes traveling on a dry, dusty path that slipped under Interstate 280 and reached as far as Felt Lake. On these walks, I developed a project called *The Slow Learning Movement: Deep Engagement for the Sake of Transformative Education.* The project was an attempt to bring lessons from the desert into my classroom, specifically into my undergraduate course, *Religion Gone Wild: Spirituality and the Environment.* The challenge was to give my students the opportunity for the course material to make deep claims on their lives, to pose transformative questions of them.

First, I adopted desert time. I slowed down the pace of the course—both literally and figuratively—in order to create a gracious sense of time and space that was conducive to deep engagement. I avoided creating a hectic syllabus comprising a vast number of topics and voluminous reading assignments. This in itself was surprisingly challenging. Assuming more is more, I had acquired the bad habit of trying to cover in a semester what had taken me decades to learn.

Mainly, however, I slowed the course down by employing a variety of approaches and principles that contributed to an ethos of deep engagement and therefore transformative education. These approaches and principles included varying the location of class meetings; paying attention to space; allowing more time for discussion (at least doubling the time); attempting to model deep listening for the students; offering an occasional contemplative exercise that focused on a particular course theme or question; and concluding the semester with a class retreat, offering suitable time and space to discuss the broader significance of students' journeys in the course. Mostly, I trusted the students, for they are courageous and competent. Generally speaking, they already know how to listen and engage thoughtfully and deeply—and they can *lead* the class (including its professor) to new vistas. They just need an opening.

Barry Lopez knows all about what I am calling the transformative or religious aspect of education—about its transcendence and its relation to reverence. One summer evening in Alaska's "late-night sun," he took a walk among the animals of the tundra in the western Brooks Range. He saw arctic birds with their vulnerable, warm eggs beneath them. All embryonic life is vulnerable, but these eggs seemed especially so, with their inward silent growth on the hard frozen ground: frail, unbending, replete eggs. What are we to do in the presence of these feral birds and fragile eggs, illuminated in the soft, pure light of the midnight sun? Lopez says that he "took to bowing on these evening walks."[73]

Lopez qualifies: "I would bow slightly with my hands in my pockets. . . ." This is not the form of worship that takes place in the high liturgy. I remember the time I nervously approached the solemn Greek priest for communion and he proclaimed in a loud voice for all the congregation to hear, "My son, you are about to receive the body and blood of Christ, and *your hands are in your pockets*!" We can hardly approach the burning bush or the Greek Orthodox priest with our everyday posture. Still, there is something in Lopez's response that is solemn, respectful, and even reverent. Foregoing formal observance, Lopez offers prayerful attentiveness and openness to wonderment.

After 228 pages of documenting in painstaking detail the varieties of Arctic light, soil, plants, animals, and human cultures, and after having reflected deeply on the complex relations between these, Lopez writes:

> Whatever evaluation we finally make of a stretch of land, no matter how profound or accurate, we will find it inadequate. The land retains an identity of its own, still deeper and more subtle than we can know.[74]

These words may dishearten some. Who wants to hear of our eternally inadequate vision and judgment? Yet with these frank words, Lopez names a land's transcendence and autonomy, its ability to make us bow in reverence. *Transcendent*, not because we find it mysteriously ineffable or ethereal, but because we can never entirely represent it in our latest vocabulary; *autonomous*, not because we cannot affect it, but because we cannot radically control it. We stand (or bow) in relation to the land, and the land enjoys its own identity and agency.

Our educational journey is the same: we must endeavor to name—represent, describe, explain—our world, even as we acknowledge the inadequacy of our names. Sometimes we must be silenced by what we study. And this, in turn, requires careful listening. The capacities to listen and to respond appropriately are as necessary for the poet as for the scientist. These interdisciplinary skills belong to transformative education.

"But there's a Tree, of many, one." That's a line from the Wordsworth poem that Paul quoted to me when I told him about the tree. In the late fall after returning from the desert, when all the trees except for the white oak had released their leaves, I came upon a tree that seemed to pose a question—a fundamental inquiry—to me. I know how this sounds. "Cladis used to be a sensible enough person, but then he experienced a personal crisis, went into the desert searching for answers, and now he's having conversations with trees." It probably won't help my case to explain that it was the *tree* that initiated our association. But I'm not claiming it was a conversation. Conversation implies a dialogue. I wasn't talking to the tree, except to exclaim now and then, "What? What? *What*?" And the tree wasn't talking to me; it stood there—unflappable, silent, yet commanding.

Here's how it all started. One day I was walking home, I came upon a tree, and it seized my attention. Somehow, its presence intimated, *to your life I pose a question.* The tree confronted me with a pressing, albeit indistinct, matter. This continued for about a year through winter's snow, spring's blossoms, summer's heat, and back into fall's crisp yellowness. It was neither a cheerful nor an aesthetic experience. Although the tree was graceful and elegant, it appeared mostly intricate and severe. This tough, medium-sized dogwood had some business with me, and it was not going to release me until it was satisfied.

"But there's a Tree, of many, one." Wordsworth's "Ode: Intimations of Immortality" is a poem about loss and renewal:

> —But there's a Tree, of many, one,
> A single Field which I have looked upon;
> Both of them speak of something that is gone.[75]

Wordsworth's grief and rebirth were not the same as mine. But I couldn't help but think that Paul, by drawing my attention to the poem, had shown me a clue to the nature of the question that the tree posed to me. The tree, like the poem, was asking about the maturation and redemption of grief—my grief. The form of the question and my response to it gradually emerged over the course of that year. It was the most powerful questioning yet about my past and future, about letting go and moving forward. And this questioning, as it turned out, was timely. It was urgent. For soon after I first encountered the tree, the opportunity of a lifetime presented itself to me. I now know that if I had lingered much longer with my grief, if I had clung to my earlier life, my own rebirth would have been postponed, perhaps forever.

Today in my office, there hangs a pen and ink drawing of the tree. Mina, the woman from Seattle who would become my wife, commissioned a Vassar student to draw it. It was her first present to me. At the time, although she had heard me allude to the tree, she could not have known the significance of the tree, could not have known that the tree stood as a bridge that allowed her life to reach mine. But there in my office is the tree, and below it are photos of Mina and our three children, Sabine, Luke, and Olive. To my eyes, these form a constellation of beauty and grace. And when I reflect on the path that led me to that group of stars, I arrive at the last line of Wordsworth's Ode, "Thoughts that do often lie too deep for tears."

The Sketch of the Tree

❧

Where have I arrived, more than ten years after the Southwest trip? I searched for a course, one for Vassar and one for myself. What have I found and kept? What have I left behind?

I thought I was searching for something like answers. In fact, I mainly discovered questions. I thought I was searching for order. Instead, I discovered chaos—yet this chaos promised re-creation. I thought I was searching for a Way. In fact, a tumultuous but life-affirming flow of events—a different kind of perfect storm—buoyed me. Kierkegaard allegedly said, "Life must be lived forwards, but it can only be understood backwards." When I look back, what do I understand?

I understand that many of the questions that once pained and dogged me seemed eventually to dissolve in love, life, and exhaustion. The questions—whose "answers" were located in the very journey of working out the questions themselves and which then seemed to disappear wholly—were no doubt central to my search. They instilled longing, they led to wonder, they posed the bigger questions—Who am I? Where have I been? Where am I heading? What am I to leave behind? What am I to keep? What is the way back to beauty? They inflicted an aching desire to find my way home.

I am grateful for the questions and for the journey. Maybe I needed those questions posed, if for no other reason than to be reminded how few answers I possessed. Surely the questions will recur, will surface again in some form at some time. But for now I can say that the haunting is all but gone. The ache has largely healed.

What chased off the ghosts? You might think that a book titled, *In Search of a Course*, as it comes to a close, would at least whisper some enlightened answers. It must disappoint then. In these pages I wrote of haunting questions and profound longings. Yet in my life—a life now shared with my spouse, children, and friends—the journey led me *through* such questions. And while I understand the likelihood of their return, they have quieted in the midst of a seemingly endless succession of professional and family tasks—teaching that new course, advising those graduate students, writing the overdue article, attending that faculty meeting; wiping up that milk, picking up this duck, crouching for hide-'n-seek behind the chair, reading *Curious George* again and again as if caught in Nietzsche's eternal recurrence, knowing that I cannot rest, cannot stop but must push on, for these *Formidable Presences*, my children, do not pause except for those occasional intervals of sleep.

In the midst of this relentless cyclone a line from Thomas Hardy comes to me: "My ponies are tired, and I have further to go."[76] In that moment I pause and even smile, for my toil has been given a name, and I know that my life is overflowing with meaning.

I have always sensed a nameless presence in my life. I have often suspected that there was a connection between this presence and the indistinct questions. At this moment, however, it seems right to say that the presence has surrounded me with a grace that comes with names I can speak and faces I can touch. Does this sound sentimental—a man saved by the love of spouse, children, and friend? I assure you: there is little that is romantic about my life or the lives of people like me. The challenges of daily life do not permit it. I have aimed for honesty in these pages in the hope that accuracy will save this book from narcissism. For if I get it right, others will see themselves—and not only me—in these pages. So here is another honest statement: In the midst of daily life, when I am utterly exhausted and sleep-deprived, I will on occasion step back, look at my life and its considerable encumbrance, and, while taking stock of this swirling chaos, delight in *this* life, and know *where* and *who* I am, and understand that I would not choose to be anyone or anywhere else. My journey is no longer in the distant desert. It is the daily trek within my home, city, and classroom.

> Journal Entry: Christmas
>
> *I hope you get what you want.* That's what the dean said to me last week. *I already have it,* I replied.
>
> And yet I ask for more. Mina and I long for another child. But how to ask appropriately? How to ask for more while acknowledging that our life is replete as it now stands? I must walk a tightrope anchored in gratitude on one side and yearning on the other. If a Child comes, she comes as a Gift. That's the Christmas story. To hold everything dear as a Gift.

About two years after writing that journal entry, Mina and I once again entered the ultrasound room. Would we find a heartbeat? The path to a second child had been difficult. Miscarriage, ectopic pregnancy, countless negative home pregnancy tests. Each month, elevated hope was drowned by menstrual blood. What image, what news, would the ultrasound bring this time? The lights dimmed, the tension rose, and then there on the bright screen was not one heart beating, but two. Twins. Our first glimpse of Olive and Luke.

Family man. That's what I have become. Have I sold out? Embraced ease and comfort? What of that line from Emerson, "People wish to be settled; only as far as they are unsettled is there any hope for them"?[77] Have I settled for settled? Early in our courtship—on its second day!—I sent that Emerson quotation to Mina. I knew our relationship would introduce chaos and discomfort into our lives, and I was probably hoping that Emerson would assure her that chaos can be needful. But what happens when, having made it through the chaotic and turbulent days of the courtship, we marry, have children, and acquire some stability? Have I shut out any hope for growth and change? It's a fair question, but one I almost never ask myself, because *I am unsettled daily.* You want to see a life turned upside down? You want to see chaos and uncertainty? Any one of my children can recreate my world, sometimes hourly. Foucault writes brilliantly of the power of social institutions to discipline the self. But he missed a significant source of power: the power of infants and toddlers to command and reorganize the world around them, especially the world of their caregivers. Anything we love has this power—certainly a spouse, but also a friend, a pet, a community, or a stretch of land.

At the end of his essay, "Ktaadn," Thoreau reflects on the wild in the natural world by comparing it to the domesticated world of museums, where objects that have been ripped from their natural context are put tidily on display:

> Talk of mysteries! Think of our life in nature,—daily to be shown matter, to come in contact with it,—rocks, trees, wind on our cheeks! the *solid* earth! the *actual* world! the *common sense! Contact! Contact! Who* are we? *where* are we?[78]

I know what it is to ache for contact. Some time ago, on long, solo car trips, I would look out the window at the distant trees and rocks, and I would wonder if in fact they were really there. Lack of contact caused me to doubt the reality outside my own skin. And then, somewhat to my own surprise, I would abruptly stop and get out of the car, jump over some fence—often at dusk—and run for a tree or large rock to touch with my hands. Like a doubting Thomas, I needed to know, *Can this be for real?* That's what I longed for, what I stood in need of: contact with a reality outside me that could remake me. We live far from such contact, such solidity, and yet we hunger for it. I now know, however, that this contact, the kind with the power to educate us deeply about *who* and *where* we are, can be occasioned by who and what we love and not only by savage mountaintops or roadside trees. I have made contact! I have experienced the wild! I know the wilderness where it reigns: it is in my home and it howls daily. The domestic can be one of the wildest places in the universe. Making contact with the wild in my household reminds me of my name and my place.

My journey to the desert ultimately led me home—to the familiar and the wild at the southern edge of the Blackstone Valley in Rhode Island. It led me to the sights and sounds of angels in the hum of everyday life. Yes, I now believe in angels, even if my own are hopelessly fallen. Our angels may be erratic and demanding, messy and noisy. They may cry or even scream. But they are real and they visit our lives with grace. They bring us to our knees in the profoundest prayers of gratitude. These angels are not the cherubs or putti of Italian Renaissance art. They are not nearly so tame. They disrupt. They thwart. They spoil our plans and our pursuit of order. They make claims. They wield power. And yes, they make *announcements*—revelatory messages. Over and over again they announce, *Your life will not go as you planned, for it is no longer strictly your own.* In response, you will at times curse your angels as demons. But in your best moments, when you are most yourself, you will bless them and be grateful for their weighty encumbrance that keeps you grounded. The angels call to us, *Allow us into your life. Allow our disruptive presence to bring you solidity and contact.*

Whatever their shape or size, all angels come with a similar mission: to save us from ourselves by making claims on us. To receive their blessing—their commanding love—we relinquish control and surrender to them. There is nothing altruistic or selfless about such surrender. On the contrary, in so doing, we open ourselves to life and love.

I believe, then, in angels. I believe in crossings to safety. Angels, of course, cannot guarantee safety. My spouse and children are not that safe. I know that now. Who in this world has greater potential to crush me than my wife and children? One or more of them could be taken from me in the length of time it takes me to write this sentence.

A *crossing* to safety, in contrast, is something we cannot be robbed of. The crossing may connect us to particular loves, a partner or child or friend. And perhaps the crossing is granted by the highest form of love, namely, Love Itself. Be that as it may, traveling over the bridge requires profound trust in the journey itself. The journey, we know, will not be without pain or chaos. Even some of our angels may, for reasons of their own, forsake us. But the journey itself is trustworthy. Its span is great and full of grace, even if each individual step does not seem safe. There will be times when a resigned acceptance is our primary task in life. We will repeat and cling to the mantra, *Keep your mind in hell, and despair not.* But today, still bathed in the new light of this dawn, the threat of despair in my life seems distant (of its actual proximity, God knows). I searched for a course and I was found by a way I could trust. And so today I will not speak of keeping my mind in hell, but of placing my heart in love and trust. Today I choose to believe that I am, ultimately, safely in love. I will save the sensible mantra for some other day.

Recently I received the following email from Ben Barney:

> Yesterday morning I went outside and sat on a bench in the warm sunlight with the four dogs lying around. I sat there and looked at the red cliffs and the darker top parts. I looked and imagined my family having been here for hundreds of years. Many generations of relatives have walked and lived in this area. I thought about their lives, what they did, and their passing on. Now here I am, sitting on a bench and thinking of them and their history and feeling a certain connection to the place and its history. This makes me less singular and less aimless. Then I think of the time in the future when someone else will remember me and I will be elsewhere. It is at such times that I feel connected in ways that make me more human. It is times like these that make my loneliness, my complicated self,

> my wants and needs, and my continual search disappear. It also makes me want to be alone and live a life that will create holiness.

Ben has his own crossings to safety. And apparently my search isn't the only one to end in its own inexplicable *disappearance.* This must happen all the time, this waxing and waning of our quests. Ben writes of his desire to be alone, but not to be disconnected or "singular." Ben has made contact. He, too, is surrounded by angels—in the red cliffs, the dogs, the ghosts of relatives, and in holiness. We all have openings for angels in our lives. Angels abound. A partner, a child, a best friend—I have named my archangels. These kinds of angels, I know, are not for everyone. They are not all Ben's. Nor are they all Paul's. Paul has no children. Instead, he has cats—about thirty of them. Feline angels—they, too, may administer works of grace as they make their claims. All these angels that have fallen into our lives arrive with profound needs and vulnerabilities. What makes them angels is not the span of their wings or the generosity in their hearts. It is their exquisite placement in our lives. It is what they offer us—the opportunity to care deeply, to love a being for its own sake, to work so that it may flourish. This burden is our salvation.

Who can doubt that there is a connection between making contact with our angels and achieving holiness? Ben is making contact and in that contact growing in holiness—he is becoming *whole.* If our wholeness depends on such contact, we must come to terms with the idea that we, too, are angels. We administer to those around us by joining them in their journeys, by caring for them and allowing them to care for us. We show up and are unreservedly *there.* We may not be pretty and we certainly aren't perfect, but we are *present.*

Contrary to popular belief, angels on earth are not in disguise. We've just been deceiving ourselves about their appearance. We search for unearthly, distant Beings who can save us from our painful lives because, presumably, they themselves do not suffer. We've convinced ourselves that the angelic face is the painless one. I write of a different class of angels. Their faces register pain—and much else as well. Their ability to save us is not measured by their distance from us, but by their proximity. Their wings may be tiny and frail and their halos flickering and dim, but these conspicuously limited beings are ours, traveling with us as we jointly make our way.

And so I went into the desert in search of a course, one for Vassar and one for myself. Yet the two became one, and instead of finding the course, I was found. The Latin word for "course" is *curriculum*, originally meaning the *current* of a river; later it came to mean the *path* of a running or chariot race; and later still, the *course* or *flow* of an education and a life. *Life's current.* Mine knocked me down and then swept me up. Yet no one is a passive vessel in the stream of life. We all must row.

Today I ask my students: What is your course? What gifts do you possess and what will you do with them—on this day? What angels are in your life and what variety of angel are you becoming? The course in the university and the course in life become one and the same. *Life's curriculum.*

Recently I was reading E.B. White's *Charlotte's Web* to Sabine when we came upon the concluding lines: "Wilbur never forgot Charlotte…. It is not often that someone comes along who is a true friend and a good writer. Charlotte was both."

Paul is both, I noted to Sabine. My children know Paul. Although neither he nor my (unbaptized) children know it, he is their spiritual godparent. My hope is that during their actual and online visits, my children are being christened in Paul's wise and gentle nature, and that later they will recite his verse, a verse that speaks of the largeness of life and the solemn ways of love and acceptance.

Paul *is* a true friend and a good writer. We maintain regular contact. When he is not residing in Warwick, New York, he lives on top of a volcano in Australia (but of course he does). Since volcanoes, too, have internet access nowadays, I can reach Paul even there. We also stay in touch by team-teaching a course—still, despite the fact that we now teach at different institutions, hundreds of miles apart. We kept this fact a strict secret until the day Paul exposed me to his students. Here is how Noah, a Vassar student, described the revelation:

> I am in a class that is team-taught, but I've never met one of my teachers. "Imagine," said the professor who actually conducts the class, "that he's here, invisibly." He—the professor whom I know—mimed putting his arm around a man in the seat next to him. For a moment I could see my teacher's fingers mold onto a formless shoulder, his forearm resting upon an airy neck. It was the sort of image that—had the absent teacher been present—would have made for a perfect desktop snapshot. There they were, eyes twinkling, ready to embark on yet another semester of intellectual adventure and attentiveness. Only, one of them was visible and one of them was not.
>
> I wouldn't have noticed the co-teacher had he not been revealed. And yet, now that he has, I am aware of the indents and depressions left by his presence. Life is like that, I think, full of invisible absences, little divots and markings that suggest a landscape defined by process: the goings and comings, the presences and absences, the subtle tugging on a universal fabric.

Paul and I are still present, then, to each other and even to our students. Still, I miss him. I miss sipping the French roast in that real presence of his kind smile. I miss watching him glide on skis through that deep, fresh snow. I miss treading together on that firm quartz conglomerate as we hike Mohonk with our students. I miss exchanging the discreet look of awe and wonder when our student crafts that statement wise and edifying.

Paul and I stay in touch, but without touching. "The subtle tugging on a universal fabric" led my friend to me and later away from me. Now I mostly speak to him—and love him—in silence. Still, even in the silence the friendship cares for me.

If given the opportunity to speak to past Vassar students, to the Navajo women, to Ben and Lorain, I would declare to them that while searching for a course, I was *found*—found by a spouse and children, by a home and a land, and by a small but growing community and assembly of friends. I would declare to them that while working to propel myself into the ways of home and place, a deep current *carried me* to my home and community, to my place and land—a current generated not by my effort but by the powerful, delightful, and sometimes turbulent flow of life. I do not wish to belittle my efforts or yours in the search for love, home, and place. But I cannot deny that this time love, home, and place came to me, pulling me along, lifting me up.

Bedtime rituals in our home are long and elaborate. Among the sequence of rites, each child individually receives a story and song. To my daughter Olive I sing "Michael Row the Boat Ashore." I sing it slowly, meaningfully. Neither of us is in a hurry. The last stanza, in my version at least, has become something of a barometer of how my days are going:

> River Jordan is deep and wide, hallelujah
> Milk and honey on the other side, hallelujah.

Some evenings, I admit, I yearn for the other side. I'm weary and my trials and tasks can loom long after sunset. On most evenings, however, I smile inwardly as I hold Olive and chant that last stanza. I'm on the other side. I'm holding the milk and honey.

We never quite arrive, of course. The Promised Land of milk and honey, I know, is not a place. It is a longing, a moving, a working, a striving, a releasing, a receiving. Still, on most evenings when I sing to Olive, I exult in my arrival. This book is the story of a journey to the other side. I will journey again and again, I know. The movement from dying to living anew is *recurrent,* an unending course. But on this evening, with this child, I allow myself to give thanks for crossing the river, deep and wide.

Acknowledgments

"When I receive a new gift, I do not macerate my body to make the account square, for, if I should die, I could not make the account square. The benefit overran the merit the first day, and has overran the merit ever since."

– Emerson, "Experience"[79]

Many have contributed to this book, and I offer them my profound gratitude. Maggie Millner, my editor, is the brilliant poet who brought her extraordinary heart and mind, her perceptive eye and ear to every sentence in this book. Without the help of Maggie, *In Search of a Course* would be a rough draft on a hard drive. Regal House Publishing manifested all the virtues of a stellar press dedicated to promoting the literary endeavors of its authors. In particular, I am grateful to the editor-in-chief, Jaynie Royal, for her the robust support, and to the senior editor, Pam Van Dyk, for her expert editing and the care that she brought to the production of the book.

Mina Cladis and Paul Kane are lifelong companions who, in my hour of greatest need, offered the strength of love and took down my grave house, stone by stone. A portion of my acknowledgement to them is detailed in these pages, as is my gratitude to Ben Barney, Lorain Fox Davis, and William and Vida Clift—my escorts and educators in the desert.

I am indebted to Erin Edmison, the first person to read an early draft, and to Jennifer Lyons, the first person to read the subsequent draft. Erin and Jennifer are wise and caring literary agents who encouraged the philosopher hidden behind the abstract reflections to reveal himself. A few of my student assistants read and commented on various drafts of the book, and I am grateful to them for their adept work: Sarah Snydacker

Bruhn, (the late) Melissa Proctor, Joshua Kurtz, Virginia Schilder, and Emilia Sowersby. As is often the case, the students became the teachers.

The narrative of *In Search of a Course* could not include every cherished friend who has helped me on my way. If it could, there would be lengthy accounts of the warmth of the Mamiya family, the love of Sam Speers, the support of Jeffrey Stout, and the friendship of Kristen Lewis and the Benson family.

My parents, (the late) John and Jenny Cladis, were exemplars of gratitude and endeavored to teach me its ways. They are a silent but palpable presence in these pages. My siblings, Mary, Christine, and George, have each helped me on my way, in different ways at different times. My children, Sabine, Olive, and Luke, are the loves of my life. If, when old enough, they read this book, may they know that my search for a course led first to their mother and then to them, my greatest joys.

And now back to Paul and Mina, to whom this book is dedicated. At the beginning of the day when I name my blessings, they (with my children) top the list, bringing a glint of dancing light to my soul, reminding me that

Outside the open window
The morning air is all awash with angels.[80]

Endnotes

1 Alexander Herzen, *My Past and Thoughts*, trans. Constance Garnett (Berkeley: University of California Press, 1982), v.

2 Richard Rodriguez, *Hunger of Memory* (New York: Dial Press, 1982), 200.

3 Ludwig Wittgenstein, *Culture and Value* (Chicago: University of Chicago, 1984), 64.

4 Ralph Waldo Emerson, *Nature*, in *Emerson: Essays and Poems*, eds. Harold Bloom, Paul Kane, and Joel Porte (New York: *The Library of America*, 1996), 14.

5 William Wordsworth, *The Prelude*, ed. Jonathan Wordsworth, M.H. Abrams, and Stephen Gill (New York: W. W. Norton, 1979), Book 12: 151. The phrase, "disappearing line," is in 12: 148.

6 Thomas Merton, *New Seeds of Contemplation* (New York: New Directions, 1962), 104. This quotation actually begins with, "Our minds are like crows."

7 Robert Frost, "I Could Give All to Time," *The Poetry of Robert Frost*, ed. Edward Connery Lathem (New York: Henry Holt and Company, 1975), 334.

8 Cited by Shunryu Suzuki, *Not Always So* (New York: Quill, 2003), 28.

9 Ralph Waldo Emerson, "Self-Reliance," *Emerson: Essays and Poems*, eds. Harold Bloom, Paul Kane, and Joel Porte (New York: *The Library of America*, 1996), 259.

10 Percy Shelley, "In Defence of Poetry," *Shelley's Poetry and Prose*, eds D.H. Reiman and S.B. Powers (New York: Norton, 1977), 517.

11 Henry David Thoreau, *Journal* vol. 1, ed. John C. Broderick (Princeton: Princeton University Press, 1981), 171.

12 Cited in Richard Rhodes, *The Making of the Atomic Bomb* (New York: Simon and Shuster, 1986), 571–572.

13 Emerson, "Experience," in *Ralph Waldo Emerson: Essays and Poems*, eds. Harold Bloom, Paul Kane, and Joel Porte (New York: Library of America, 1996), 491.

14 Terry Tempest Williams, *An Unspoken Hunger* (New York: Vintage Books, 1994), 86.

15 Henry David Thoreau, *Journal* vol. 9 (August 30, 1856), ed. Bradford Torrey and Francis H. Allen (New York: Dover, 1962), 43.

16 Henry David Thoreau, "Walking," in *The Portable Thoreau* (New York: Penguin Books, 1982), 609.

17 Plato, *Symposium*, trans. Robin Waterfield (Oxford: Oxford University Press, 1994), 30.

18 Thich Nhat Hanh, *The Miracle of Mindfulness: A Manual on Meditation* (Boston: Beacon Press, 1987), 36.

19 Wittgenstein, *Tractatus Logico-Philosophicus*, trans. D. F. Pears and B. F. McGuinness (London: Routledge and Kegan Paul, 1961), 74.

20 Mary Oliver, "Entering the Kingdom," *Twelve Moons* (Boston: Little, Brown, and Company, 1979), 21.

21 For the expression, "rooted cosmopolitanism," see Kwame Anthony Appiah, *The Ethics of Identity* (Princeton: Princeton University Press, 2007), 213 ff.

22 Wittgenstein, *Culture and Value*, 56.

23 Emerson, "Circles," in *Emerson: Essays and Poems*, eds. Harold Bloom, Paul Kane, and Joel Porte (New York: *The Library of America*, 1996), 413.

24 Robert Frost, "I Could Give All to Time," *The Poetry of Robert Frost*, 334.

25 Lao Tzu, *Tao Te Ching*, trans. Victor Mair (NY: Bantam Books, 1990), 21 (15 [52]).

26 Quoted by Barry Pritzker, in *Ansel Adams* (New York: Crescent Books, 1991), 91.

27 William James, *The Varieties of Religious Experience* (New York: Penguin, 1985), 104.

28 Helen and Scott Nearing, *The Sugar Maple Book* (New York: John Day Company, 1950), 238.

29 Simone Weil, "Forms of the Implicit Love of God," in *Waiting for God*, trans. Emma Craufurd (New York: Harper and Row, 1973), 210.

30 Paul Kane, *Drowned Lands* (Columbia: University of South Carolina Press, 2000), 74.

31 Percy Shelley, "To Wordsworth," in *Shelley's Poetry and Prose*, ed. Donald Reiman and Neil Fraistat, (New York: Norton, 2002), 92, lines 1-2.

32 Percy Shelley, "Mont Blanc: Lines Written in the Vale of Chamouni," in *Shelley's Poetry and Prose*, 99, lines 76-81.

33 "Keep your mind in hell, and despair not" is the epigraph to Gillian Rose's *Love's Works* (New York: Schocken, 1995).

34 Thomas Merton, *New Seeds of Contemplation*, 13.

35 Paul Kane, *Drowned Lands*, 6.

36 Robert Frost, *The Poetry of Robert Frost*, 29-30.

37 Robert Frost, *The Poetry of Robert Frost*, 105.

38 Paul Kane, *Drowned Lands*, 6.

39 Wallace Stegner, *Crossing to Safety* (New York: Penguin, 1988), 201.

40 *Wisdom of the Buddha: The Unabridged Dhammapada*, trans. Max Muller (New York: Dover, 2000), 38 (chapter 22: 313).

41 John Dewey, *The Quest for Certainty* (New York: Minton, Balch, and Company, 1929), 302.

42 Mary Oliver, *The Leaf and the Cloud* (U.S.A.: Da Capo Press, 2000), 48-49.

43 Frederick Sommer, *Venus, Jupiter and Mars: The Photographs of Frederick Sommer*, ed. John Weiss (Wilmington: Delaware Art Museum, 1980), 18.

44 Hannah Hinchman, *A Trail Through Leaves: The Journal as a Path to Place* (NY: Norton, 1999), 15.

45 Leslie Marmon Silko, "Landscape, History, and the Pueblo Memory," in *At Home on the Earth: Becoming Native to Our Place*, ed. David Landis Barnhill (Berkeley: University of California Press, 1999), 30.

46 T. E. Hulme, "Romanticism and Classicism," in *T.E. Hulme: Selected Writings* (NY: Routledge, 2003), 78.

47 Annie Dillard, *The Writing Life* (New York: Harper, 1990), 72-73.

48 For the most part, this written version of the oral telling of the North-West Native American story is by David Wagoner, *Traveling Light* (University of Illinois Press, 1999), 10; I have made some slight changes based on the oral versions that I have heard.

49 John Dewey, *Experience and Nature* (New York: Dover, 1958), 38.

50 Terry Tempest Williams, *An Unspoken Hunger*, 134.

51 Plato, *Republic*, trans. Tom Griffith (Cambridge: Cambridge University Press, 2000), 34 (352D).

52 Aristotle, *The Basic Works of Aristotle,* ed. Richard McKeon (New York: Random House, 1941), 953 (1103b27-28).

53 Charles Dickens, *Hard Times* (New York: Walter J. Black, Inc., 1950), 2-3.

54 Thomas Huxley, "Science and Culture," in *English Literature and its Background* vol. 2 (New York: Hold, Rinehart and Winston, 1962), 778.

55 Matthew Arnold, *Culture and Anarchy*, (Whitefish, MT: Kessinger Publishing, 2004), 3.

56 See Matthew Arnold, "Literature and Science," *Matthew Arnold*, eds. Miriam Allott and Robert Super (Oxford: Oxford University Press, 1986), 468.

57 Henry David Thoreau, "Walking," 612-613.

58 Emerson, "The American Scholar," in *Emerson: Essays and Poems*, eds. Harold Bloom, Paul Kane, and Joel Porte (New York: *The Library of America*, 1996), 59.

59 Emerson quoting Caliph Ali, in "Self-Reliance," 281.

60 *A Slant of Light* is the title of one of Paul Kane's collections of poems (Victoria: Whitmore Press, 2008). The title comes from Emily Dickinson's poem, "A Slant of Light."

61 Paul Kane, "Acceptance," in *Drowned Lands*, 6.

62 Annie Dillard, *Pilgrim at Tinker Creek* (New York: Perennial Classics, 1998), 17.

63 Denise Levertov "Conversion of Brother Lawrence," *The Stream and the Sapphire* (New York: New Directions Books, 1997), 46.

64 Denise Levertov, *The Stream and the Sapphire*, 18.

65 See Doug Brugge, Timothy Benally, Esther Yazzie-Lewis, eds., *The Navajo People and Uranium Mining* (Albuquerque: University of New Mexico Press, 2006), xvii-xviii; 2-5; 89-115.

66 Robert Frost, "A Servant to Servants," in *The Poetry of Robert Frost*, ed. Edward Connery Lathem (New York; Henry Holt, 1969), 67-68, lines 171-77.

67 Wittgenstein, *Culture and Value*, 53.

68 Robert Frost, "A Line-storm Song," in *The Poetry of Robert Frost*, ed. Edward Connery Lathem (New York; Henry Holt, 1969), 27, lines 31-32.

69 Wittgenstein, *Culture and Value*, 76.

70 Thoreau, "Walking," 772.

71 Rainer Maria Rilke, *Rilke on Love and Other Difficulties*, trans. John Mood (New York: Norton: 1994), 34.

72 John Donne, "Holy Sonnets," in *The Poems of John Donne,* ed. Herbert Grierson (Oxford: Claredon Press, 1912), XXVII, 347.

73 Barry Lopez, *Arctic Dreams* (New York: Vintage, 2001), xx.

74 Barry Lopez, *Arctic Dreams*, 228.

75 Wordsworth's "Odd: Intimations of Immortality from Recollections of Early Childhood," in *English Literature* vol. II, eds. Bernard Grebanier, Samuel Middlebrook, Stith Thompson, and William Watt (NY: Holt, Rinehart, and Winston, 1962), 176.

76 Thomas Hardy, *The Return of the Native* (New York: Dover, 2003), 7.

77 Emerson, "Circles," in *Emerson: Essays and Poems*, eds. Harold Bloom, Paul Kane, and Joel Porte (New York: *The Library of America*, 1996), 413.

78 Henry David Thoreau, "Ktaadn" in *The Wilderness Reader*, ed. Frank Bergon (Reno: University of Nevada Press, 1980), 135.

79 Emerson, "Experience," 491.

80 Purdy Wilbur, *Richard Wilbur: Collected Poems 1943-2004* (New York: Harcourt, 2004), 307.